PRINT CASEBOOKS 3/THIRD ANNUAL EDITION
THE BEST IN COVERS & POSTERS

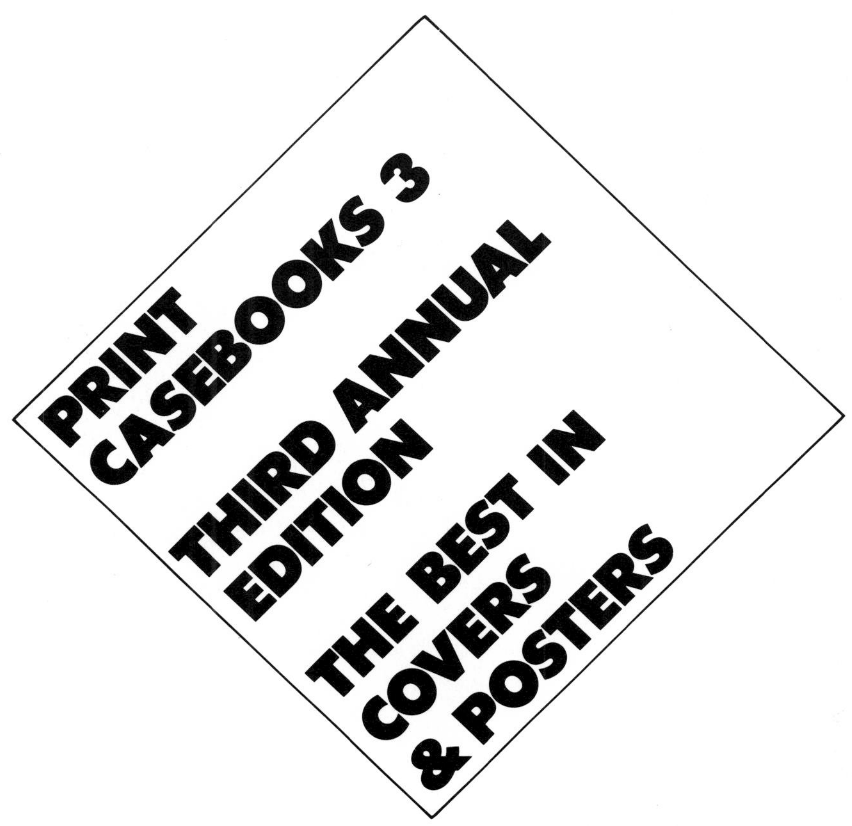

Conceived by
Martin Fox

Text and Introduction by
Carol Stevens Kner

Published by
RC Publications, Inc.
Washington, D.C.

INTRODUCTION

Published by RC Publications, Inc.
6400 Goldsboro Road NW
Washington, D.C. 20034

Manufactured in U.S.A.
First Printing 1978

PRINT CASEBOOKS 3/THIRD ANNUAL EDITION/THE BEST IN COVERS & POSTERS
Library of Congress Catalog Card Number 75-649580
ISBN 0-915734-24-9

PRINT CASEBOOKS 3/THIRD ANNUAL EDITION
Complete 6-Volume Set
ISBN 0-915734-18-4

RC PUBLICATIONS
President and Publisher: Robert Cadel
Vice President and Editor: Martin Fox
Art Director/Designer: Andrew P. Kner
Associate Editor: Teresa Reese
Associate Art Director: Carol Stevens Kner
Business Manager: Howard Cadel
Title Page Illustration: Isadore Seltzer

In 17th-century France, it was easy to tell the good art from the bad. Masterpieces worthy of official recognition and approval were voted a place of honor in the Salon d'Apollon by members of the French Academy. This élite body had established beyond a shadow of a doubt the official criteria for determining the merit of any given work of art. Paintings which didn't measure up were simply refused. The Academy's authority was such that it took almost two centuries for a group of anti-establishment artists to join forces and take part in an opposition exhibit for rejected works.

Endorsing undisputed excellence in 20th-century graphic design—putting together a Casebook of graphic solutions which can truly be called *the best*—is not so easy. There are more artists and more competitions and very little sense of the inevitable superiority of any particular selection of designs. One show's winner is relegated to another show's *salon des refusés*. A survey of selected pieces from Art Directors Club shows throughout the country, the various AIGA exhibits, the STA show in Chicago, the CA Annual and the Print Casebooks reveals surprisingly few repeats.

The burden for this changeable cast of winners falls naturally on the tenets of a democratic society (an authoritarian Academy with rigid rules and regulations would be unthinkable) and the variable panels of jurors chosen to review the shows. It would be simple enough to assess any given competition by Bauhaus standards, for example, or even the more eclectic principles of a studio like Push Pin, but nobody wants to. Juries are selected with an eye to examining competing designs with the best possible balance of opinions. One juror's specialty offsets another's. It is essential that each member of a jury view the work from the unique vantage point of his own good taste and professional experience, that he be able to compromise between his private sympathies and his understanding of the field from an objective point of view.

Further confusing the issue of what is *best* in any given year is the complex process of judging. With no standardized guidelines and an enormous variety of entries to review, the task of the jury is beset with difficulties. To begin with, a juror's attitude may be colored by circumstances of a mundane and personal nature. The weather is dreadful and he couldn't find a cab. He left an unsolved problem at the office that interferes with his concentration. He feels intimidated by one of the other jurors.

On a less subjective level, there is the overwhelming quantity of material he is being asked to consider. The very number of entries diminishes the impact of any one piece. How can he stave off the inevitable numbness that begins to take hold after the first couple of hours?

Determining the relative merits of dissimilar items is also troublesome. The only truly fair competition is one in which the problem is the same for all entrants. PRINT magazine's student cover design competition is a case in point: each competitor deals with the same market, the same budget, and the same format; talent is the only variable. Major design shows accept entries which are far more diverse. Can a magazine cover saddled with a standard format, a mass market, and any number of required lines of copy compete fairly with the cover of a museum catalog sold in a gallery book shop to a select, sophisticated audience?

Can a jury be expected to assess the work reliably without knowing the problems the designer had to cope with? "If you had that information," Richard Wilde observes, "you could judge the piece by the right standards. Only if the problem is solved really well does one have a sense of what it was."

Once the juror has settled these questions to his satisfaction, it remains for him to determine his own criteria for picking the winners. Should his selection represent a cross section of good, competent work or should he restrict his choices to truly outstanding concepts that open up new perspectives for future graphic design? If he opts for the spectacular, has he damned with faint praise a perfectly adequate body of design, perhaps from less graphically sophisticated sections of the country where last year's innovative work is just beginning to have an influence? If he decides to look for the pacesetters, will he be able to find as many as ten pieces that are truly worthy of that designation?

In the end, a show is only as good as its entries. The more there are, the better are the chances that the finalists will make up an exciting collection of work. If a good choice of designs is not forthcoming, if formerly dependable entrants fail to submit their work, the competition is severely handicapped.

Taking this vexing array of considerations as a background for the Print Casebooks, can we in all honesty call this volume "The Best in Covers & Posters?" Do the pieces really represent the excellence implied by the title? From the point-of-view of a French Academy, the answer is probably no; but if our pluralistic society won't tolerate the jurisdiction of such an authoritative body, we must learn to understand its substitute—instead of one salon, a variety of shows each with a slightly different focus and character. To determine the best graphics in any one year, the viewer must study them all, consider the perspectives of the various jurors, and proceed to make up his own mind. To a certain extent, the best is in the eye of the beholder. If an absolute remains elusive, that is both the burden and the blessing of a free society.

The value of a Casebook lies in pointing out that there are no absolutes and in giving the reader the background on which to base his own decision. Catalogs of other major shows, which simply offer reproductions of the winning entries with credits, provide no information by which to assess a work's credentials. A dazzling album cover produced at the whim of a superstar with comparatively liberal funds is presented as the absolute equal of a dazzling book jacket put together on a limited budget and supervised by an unwieldy group of arbiters including author, editor, art director, designer, and salesmen. The Casebook presents the winners but acknowledges the unavoidable inequalities of the contest. David Lance Goines' posters are superb examples of good taste, elegant graphics and excellent printing. But the reader makes no mistake about the privacy of Goines' enterprise and his avoidance of most commercial limitations. His designs can be judged on their own merits, as can the University of California/ Berkeley's low-budget diazo posters and several glossy record albums whose original treatment suggests that the relationship of the graphics to the music is a good deal less important than the visibility of the cover in a retail display.

Once the reader understands this background, he can assess the meaning of the word *best* as it applies to this particular Casebook. It is a superlative that the Casebook jury was itself anxious to define. "There were gaps in the entries," remarks Bob Scudellari, who was disappointed in the limited showing of paperbacks and record albums (Columbia Records sent no entries at all). "It is unfair to think that the winners are judged against all possible competitors." "That shortchanged the Casebook a bit, but we picked the best of what we had," observes Walter Bernard; "a lot of work is professional and competent, but we are not in a very exciting period."

The jurors may have reason to be nostalgic about the expansive purse-strings and lively innovations of the '60s, but given the stringent nature of current design budgets and the creative caution that goes with it, they have chosen *their* best from a reasonably representative group of candidates. It remains for the reader to look through these pages and see if he agrees.

—Carol Stevens Kner

CASEBOOK JURORS

Acy R. Lehman

Not a recent year has gone by in which Acy R. Lehman, art director at RCA Records since 1970, has not had work accepted in major shows—among them, the New York Directors Club, the Society of Illustrators and AIGA. He was a Gold Medal winner in the Art Directors Club Show for 1973. Lehman studied advertising design at Pratt Institute, the New School, and the Art Students League. Before joining RCA, he was executive art director at W. H. Schneider and art director for West, Weir & Bartel. He also was an art director at Grey Advertising.

Carol Stevens Kner

This is Carol Kner's second Casebook on Covers & Posters. She is currently associate art director of PRINT magazine, as well as a staff writer. Before joining PRINT, she was a buyer of technical illustrations at Doubleday. Her writings include an essay on the history of publicity and advertising in McGraw-Hill's *Encyclopedia of World Art*. Ms. Kner graduated from Smith College with a major in Art History and studied at the Università degli Studi in Florence.

Samuel Antupit

Currently executive art director of Book-of-the-Month Club and proprietor of the Cycling Frog Press, Antupit has spent his working life in editorial design. His firm, Antupit & Others, serves as consultants and designers for book and magazine publishers, record companies and corporate publications. He was art director of Esquire from 1963-1969 and, briefly, in 1977. He designed the New York Review of Books, Foreign Policy, and Art in America. His firm's clients have included Consumer Reports, Atlantic Monthly, Random House, Viking Press and McGraw-Hill.

R.D. Scudellari

Bob Scudellari is corporate art director of Random House, Inc., representing the multi-imprint publishing houses of Random House, Alfred A. Knopf, Pantheon, Vintage Books and Modern Library. During the past ten years at Random House, Scudellari has developed and directed the firm's corporate graphics and supervised the graphics for the separate publishing divisions. Previously, he was design and/or art director at Harper & Row, Western Publishing and Dell Publishing. He has participated in the National Endowment for the Arts' graphic program evaluating governmental graphics, and is presently the publishing vice-president of AIGA.

Richard Wilde

Richard Wilde has been co-chairman of the Media Arts Department of School of Visual Arts for the past seven years, as well as art director of School of Visual Arts Publications (posters, promotional pieces, booklets, catalogs and ads). Previously, he was art director at Daniel and Charles and before that design director for Pratt Publications. His numerous awards include the Silver Award, as well as others, from the New York Art Directors Show, and the Andy Award of Distinction, along with other Andys.

Walter Bernard

Walter Bernard became art director of Time magazine in June 1977 after redesigning the publication's format. From 1968-1977 he was art director of New York magazine and before that was for four years assistant art director of Esquire. Bernard was chairman of AIGA's "Mental Picture II: Portraits" exhibition and has received awards from AIGA, the Art Directors Show, the Illustrators Show, the Society of Publication Designers, and other groups. He has taught at Cooper Union at various times since 1971.

Magazines/Book Titles/Album Titles/Poster Titles

Clients/Publishers/Record Companies

Design Firms/ Art Directors/Designers

Photographers/ Illustrators/Letterers

Macho

The title of Gabor Szabo's jazz album, *Macho,* suggested to designer Richard Mantel the perfect image for the cover design—a motorcycle engine. Regarding the splendid machine as both a symbol of power and an esthetically beautiful object, Mantel decided that an abstracted close-up of its gleaming mechanical complexity would provide just the visual excitement he wanted. The image was related to the music as well—in its acceleration and pulling back, and in its rhythm. Mantel hired a brand-new Harley-Davidson, had it delivered to John Paul Endress's studio, and let the photographer do his work. The resulting display of dazzling metal surfaces, shadowy recesses and intricate machinery is virtually tactile. Mantel credits the cover's ultimate effectiveness to truly exceptional printing, the contribution of Eastern Press in New Haven. Involving the most up-to-date laser and computer technology, their operations are regulated to provide lots of time for adjustments and corrections. The printing is done in small runs at a slow enough speed to allow for continuous supervision of quality and registration. *Macho* was a straight four-color process job, but its intensity and depth make it seem the result of a much more complicated process. The surface was liquid laminated.

Client: CTI Records
Design firm: Push Pin Studios, New York
Art director/designer: Richard Mantel
Photographer: John Paul Endress

The Tim Weisberg Band

To beat the stiff competition in the album market place, "you gotta," as the stripper says in *Gypsy*, "have a gimmick." This pragmatic attitude is responsible for a lot of visually provocative cover art which sometimes needs interpretation, at least for the uninitiated. The cover of a recent Tim Weisberg album is a case in point. Weisberg is a rock-and-roll flute player with a classical background. Most of his previous albums have featured pretty straightforward designs showing a picture of Weisberg with his flute. "This time," explains art director Ria Lewerke, "we wanted something new, something on the bizarre side, so that people who saw it would stop and look and wonder what was going on." With this end in view, Lewerke and her colleagues went to a lake near Los Angeles, hired a boat, and sent out a masked swimmer with a light, chrome-plated plastic tube. The tube represents Weisberg's collected wind instruments—a C flute, bass flute, alto flute, E-flat flute, and electric flute; it is a motif which is successfully repeated in Lewerke's airbrushed "TWB" logo.

Just in case the album has been put in the display rack backside-to, the reverse cover is equally arresting. A nurse, an indispensable member of the audience at rock concerts where first-aid may be required for over-stimulated fans, throws to the swimmer as a lifeline an unwinding roll of gauze.

Client: United Artists Records
Art director: Ria Lewerke
Photographer: Moshe Brakha

White Women

helmut newton • white women

stonehill

"There must be a certain look of availability in the women I photograph. I think the woman who gives the appearance of being available is sexually more exciting than a woman who's completely distant. This sense of availability I find erotic." So says Helmut Newton in his book *White Women*, an album of fashion and film personalities photographed with a heavy cast of bizarre sensuality. As an illustration of Newton's statement, the wrap-around cover photograph, cropped tight to give impact to an image which is sensual but not pornographic, is inspired. It is somehow less representative of the collection of pictures inside. Newton's photography celebrates erotic tableaux in lavish settings, but it is an eroticism devoid of warmth or joy. The sensuality of his pictures is laden with cool Teutonic disdain and a hint of sadism. Designed by Bea Feitler, who worked closely with the photographer in the selection and editing of the photographs, the cover radiates a warmth and almost palpable closeness not entirely characteristic of Newton's work. It was printed in Italy on Mondadori's five-color presses, and varnished.

Publisher: Stonehill Publishing
Designer: Bea Feitler
Photographer: Helmut Newton

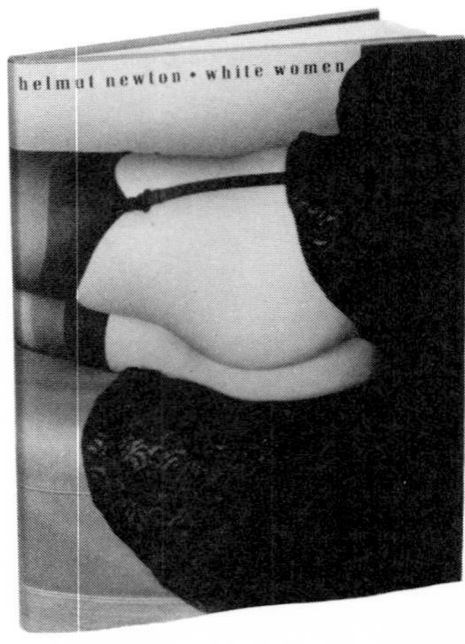

In his first novel, playwright Bob Randall *(6 Rms Riv Vu)* sticks close to familiar territory —the theater. *The Fan* chronicles the obsessive admiration of a writer of fan letters for a glamorous and successful actress. Stylistically, the book is a tour de force consisting entirely of letters from several different correspondents whose comments and descriptions serve to develop character and plot.

Paul Bacon wanted his jacket design to reflect not only the dangerous nature of the title character but also the letter motif which unifies the novel's form and content. Although his first sketch was rejected, it was probably a more interesting concept than the final art. "The jacket looked like the corner of a letter," Bacon explains. "The face of the actress was on the stamp and she was being cancelled by a postmark in the form of title and author. The trouble was that it was a little too miniature. It was difficult to make it big enough to work as a book jacket." The second, approved version—black-and-white on a silver background with a disturbing trickle of red seeping out from under the envelope—suggests the book's unusual form and the gradual unfolding horror of the story.

Client: Random House
Art director: R. D. Scudellari
Designer: Paul Bacon

Your Mind Is On Vacation

Mose Allison sings a delta blues kind of music, songs which chronicle the highs and lows of day-to-day happenings in a way that gives the ordinary person to understand that his troubles are the same as everybody else's. The titles—"Foolin' Myself," "What to Do After You Ruin Your Life," "Perfect Moment" and "No Matter"—are a roster of personal mood swings. In "Your Mind is On Vacation (and your mouth is working overtime)," the title song of this release, Allison berates the "big guys," politicians and landlords, who say one thing and mean another, or maybe say nothing at all. To illustrate Allison's reproachful comments on the album cover, art director Abie Sussman asked Seymour Chwast to depict a two-faced, cigar-smoking, heavyweight with an empty room where his brain should be. It is an image that lends itself to Chwast's broad, epigrammatic style. To save time in a tight production schedule, Sussman asked Chwast to throw in the lettering, a capriciously textured line of copy that complements the anatomical whimsy of the illustration.

Client: Atlantic Records
Art director: Abie Sussman
Designers: Abie Sussman, Seymour Chwast
Illustrator: Seymour Chwast

Suite for the Single Girl

Jerry Butler's *Suite for the Single Girl* is a rhythm-and-blues-based collection of songs describing the moods and experiences of an unmarried female. The cover design, which is considerably more subdued and to the point than the graphics for other Casebook albums, features a photograph of a grease-stained brown paper bag and a Gucci purse. It is a symbol which Helen Gurley Brown would approve of. Bring your own lunch (if you're not invited out) and spend the savings on something luxurious that will give you (and everyone else) a better image of yourself. Stanley R. Martin, who designed this Motown album, credits assistant-to-the-art director Ms. Lindsay Smith and several other co-workers with the Gucci bag idea. "Finding the right symbolism for a single woman is difficult these days," he observes; "the two bags seemed to illustrate the contrast between the reality of the single girl's status and the dream." On the back cover, the paper sack has been replaced by sunglasses, an Anne Klein scarf, travel folders and some power-of-positive-thinking reading matter.

Because Gucci was distressed to find its elegant handbag displayed with a grease-stained sack, Martin reports that the paper bag on the second edition was cleaned up.

Client: Motown Records
Art director: Carl Overr
Designer: Stanley R. Martin
Photographer: Gene Brownell

Five months after the Carter Administration took office, New York magazine published a report on the new life of former Secretary of State Henry Kissinger. Promoted with the cover line "Henry Gets His Act Together," the article was written by Tad Szulc, who summed up his piece with remarks indicating that the shrewd negotiator and diplomat with a flair for dramatic effect was preparing for an active future in the public eye. "Now only time will tell," Szulc observed, "whether and how Kissinger will re-emerge fully on the national stage."

Taking his lead from the manuscript, art director Tom Bentkowski arranged for a cover photo depicting Kissinger as an actor in his dressing room preparing to go on stage. "Much of the impact," Bentkowski remarks, "derives from the fact that we were able to find a model (Jan Leighton) who could make himself look enough like Kissinger to cause a suspension of disbelief on the part of the viewer." In fact, the art director reports, some people thought it really *was* Kissinger. Bentkowski's deadline was unusually tight. The idea was conceived on a Friday afternoon, the shot set up for Monday, and the finished cover went to the printer on Wednesday. Although he was generally satisfied with the results, Bentkowski says that, given more time, he would have had the engraving color-corrected to reduce the over-all bluish cast.

Publisher: NYM Corp.
Art director/designer: Tom Bentkowski
Photographer: Carl Fischer

Fabrics for Historic Buildings

When James Morrison was asked to design the cover for a Preservation Press publication called *Fabrics for Historic Buildings,* he was given as reference material a number of black-and-white photographs of textiles shown in the book. Produced for a market including both amateur decorators and professional restorationists, the 64-page paperback offers detailed information about the selection, ordering and installation of reproduction fabrics. It also features a catalog listing 225 reproductions of textiles used in the U.S. in the 18th century through 1900, and commercially available today through such well-known manufacturers as Brunschwig & Fils, Scalamandré, and F. Schumacher. "The book emphasizes the importance of using a fabric appropriate to the historical context of the restoration," comments associate editor Alice Bowsher; "some materials are currently available in ten colors but only one—the color of the original dye—is historically appropriate." To suggest not only the beauty of the fabrics but also the text's emphasis on authenticity, Morrison based his cover on an 18th-century resist-dyed floral pattern. Reducing the original Schumacher sample photograph to a line shot, he had the design printed in its original navy blue. The type is apple green.

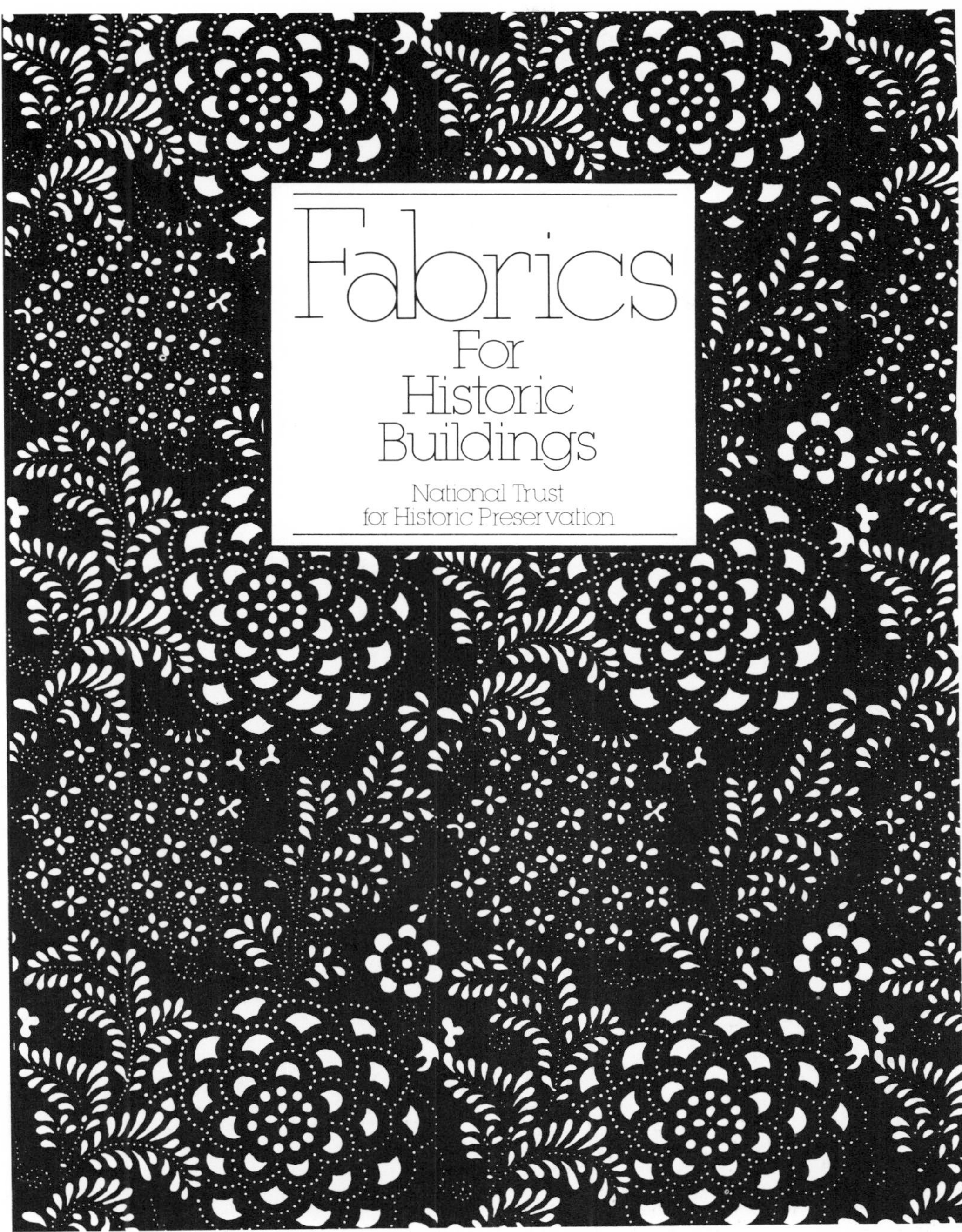

Publisher: Preservation Press, National Trust for Historic Preservation
Art director/designer: James R. Morrison

The Iron Staircase

When Wendell Minor was asked to design the cover for a Simenon mystery called *The Iron Staircase*, he was told specifically not to base his illustration on the title. Beyond that, he was supplied with the manuscript and given free rein. Simenon, of course, can be relied on for other sources of inspiration, and after reading the story, Minor found that the appropriate image stood out clearly in his mind from a blur of other possibilities.

The plot revolves around a woman who is slowly killing her husband with small doses of poison hidden in his evening meal. Although the husband is aware of his wife's treachery, he allows her murderous scheme to continue on its fatal course because he loves her so much. The summary of this unconvincing tale suggests that Minor's image of a fork as prison bars might be a good deal weightier than the fiction behind it. Subjected to the usual trade publishing obstacle course, his design easily won the approval of editor, art director, and sales department, and went on to prove itself an effective sales tool in bookstores. Minor, who feels that his first concept is usually the best, was pleased with its success.

SIMENON

The Iron Staircase

Publisher: Harcourt Brace Jovanovich
Art director: Harris Lewine
Designer/illustrator: Wendell Minor

Lonnie Liston Smith and the Cosmic Echoes produce an entirely contemporary sound, the kind of warm, vibrant rhythm that floats up from a passing transistor on a summer night—nothing to do with the subtle harmonies of 14th-century Europe. Smith, nonetheless, found "Renaissance" an appropriate name for his album. It suggested to him a universal rebirth (that would stretch the interpretations of most art historians) and, on a personal level, it symbolized his own renewed sense of artistic achievement. For art director Dick Smith and illustrator David Plourde, the word was an obvious source of inspiration for the cover art. Plourde, who enjoys the recreation of detailed realistic settings, conjured up from his imagination, in warm, muted colors and a meticulous classical style, the confines of a Renaissance painter's studio. Using photos of Smith supplied by RCA, he depicted the recording artist in 15th-century costume just finishing his self-portrait. "It's a good image," comments the art director, "because Smith paints *his* pictures through his music." As an expression of Smith's belief in the importance of a universal coming together of mankind, Dick Smith framed Plourde's painting with a border of cosmic symbols—water signs, earth signs, primitive and religious emblems—which are shown again inside the album with explanations of their meaning.

A second RCA album presents much more traditional music, a Brahms piano concerto, with a much less traditional style of illustration. "We wanted a new cover approach for material which was not new but had never before been released," explains art director Joseph Stelmach. Enlisting the talents of Miriam Brofsky, a sculptor who works in bronze, clay, epoxy, and metal, Stelmach supplied pictures of Rubenstein and Reiner and asked that she cut out portraits in flat metal which could be arranged in different positions. Brofsky submitted three 6″ by 6″ clay sketches of her ideas, one of which suggested a shiny profile against a matte-finish metal that, unfortunately, would have

Client: RCA Records
Art directors: Acy Lehman, Dick Smith
Illustrator: David Plourde

Rubenstein, Reiner, Brahms

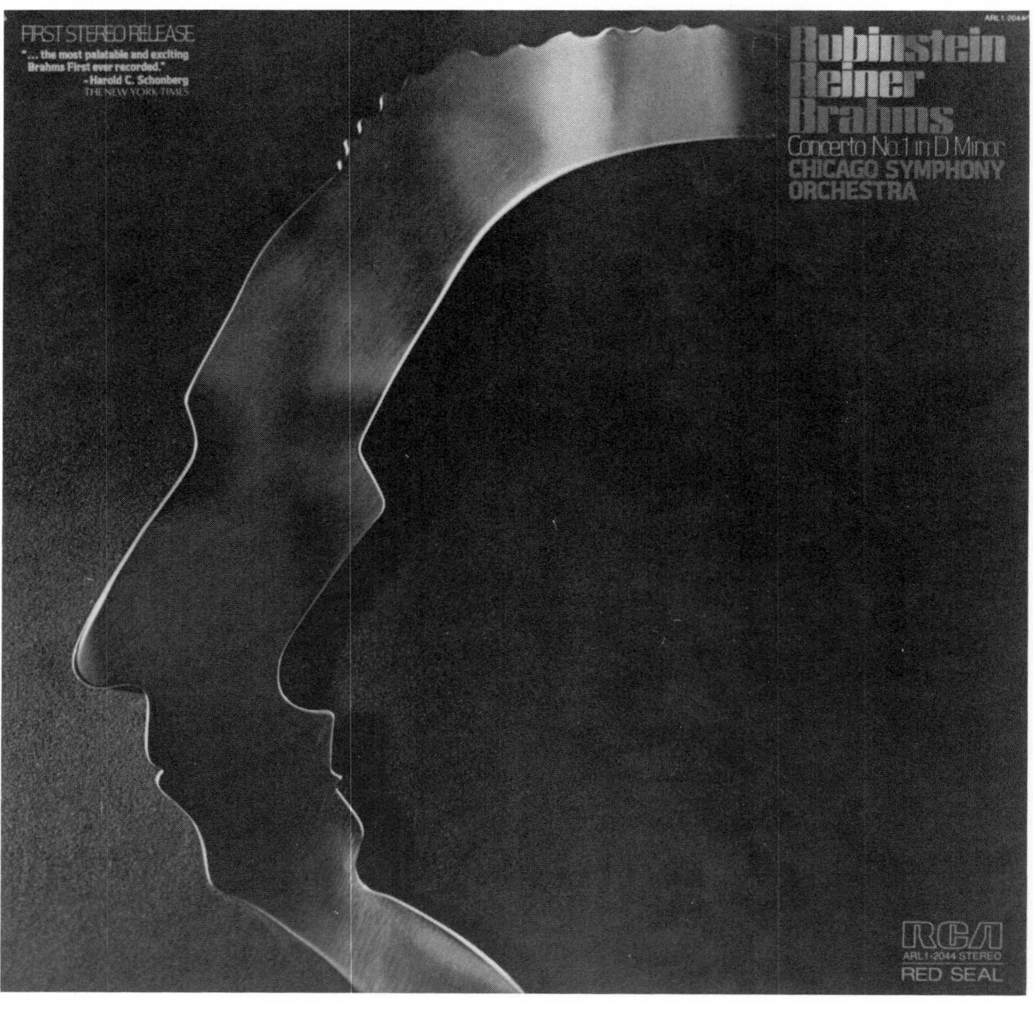

been impossible to photograph because of the reflections. Her final sculpture, however, cut out of one piece of brass with a power saw and shined by a brass polisher in Chinatown, achieves a similar effect. Photographed against black felt, Rubenstein's face appears as the positive shape and Reiner's as the negative.

Brofsky used metal again for the illustration on a Stravinsky recording performed by Peter Serkin's quartet, Tashi. Her technique this time, however, was quite different. Stelmach wanted to give this classical album a youthful image which would suggest both the age of the recording artists and the contemporary nature of the music. Following Stelmach's direction—"I want the five lines of a musical staff and somehow they become the composer's head—" Brofsky decided to use ⅛" hollow brass tubing for the lines. Fashioning Stravinsky's features out of brass wire, she mixed gold dust with epoxy and glued the wires to the tubes so that the seams wouldn't show. Then, she laboriously glued each

Client: RCA Records
Art director/designer: Joseph Stelmach
Sculpture: Miriam Brofsky
Photographer: David B. Hecht

Tashi Plays Stravinsky

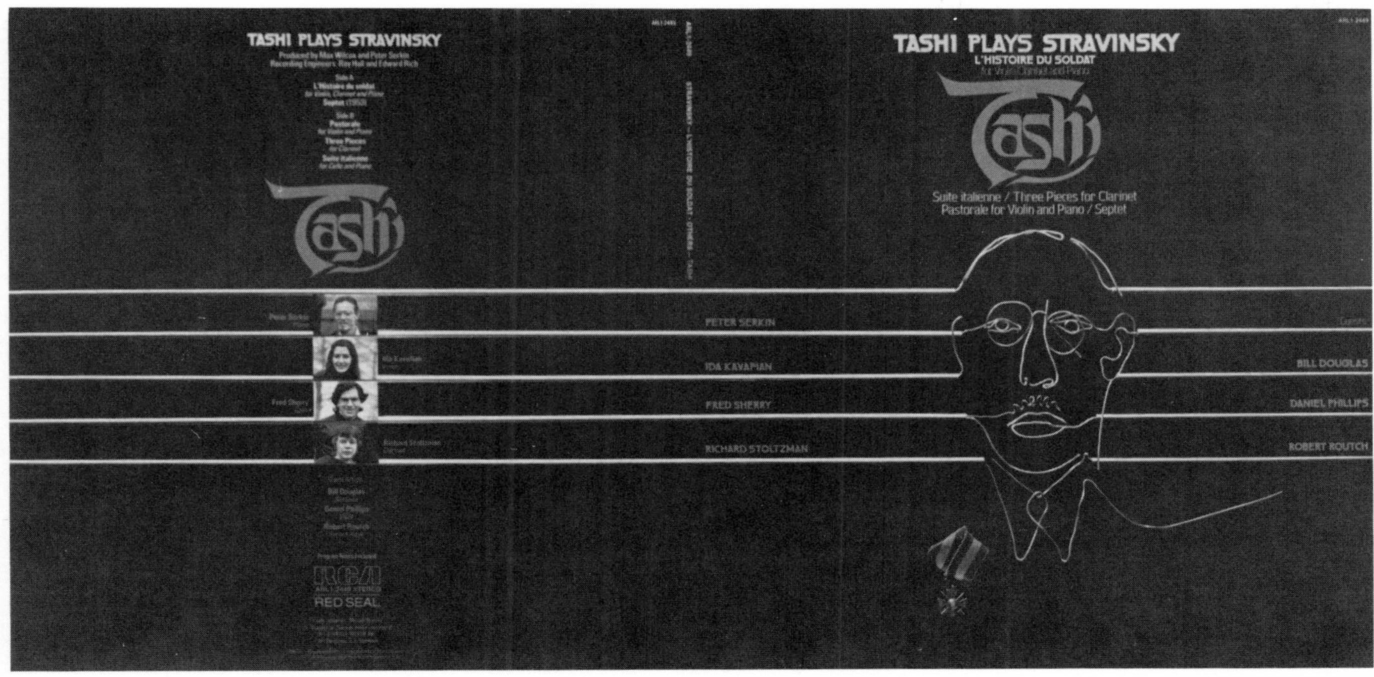

separate section of the portrait to a felt-covered board. "The hardest part was getting the tubes straight," she recalls. "They were the last things I put down and I kept feeling they would spring back into some baroque pattern." Brofsky, who usually supervises the photography of her sculpture, confidently left it to Stelmach. "He handles so much photography of collage and still-life illustration that I knew it would turn out well," she explains. The typography reflects the oriental origins of the Tibetan word "Tashi," meaning "good fortune."

Client: RCA Records
Art director/designer: Joseph Stelmach
Sculpture: Miriam Brofsky
Photographer: David B. Hecht

Say It in Private

There wouldn't seem to be much connection between French Revolutionist Jean Paul Marat, founder of the polemical anti-establishment journal L'Ami du People, and contemporary popular vocalist Steve Goodman, singer of melodies such as "You're the Girl I Love," "Video Tape," and "Weary Blues from Waitin'." And there wasn't—until art director Tony Lane decided to come down hard on record-store competition by selling the Goodman album with a cover illustration guaranteed to induce double-take reactions. With nothing to go on but some photos of the performer and a line from one of his songs—"Say it in private"—as the title, Lane was free to develop any graphic solution he liked. Eighteenth-century artist Jacques-Louis David's painting of the death of Marat offered appealing possibilities. Lane thought that Goodman's sense of humor and political awareness could be provocatively represented in a spoof of the famous work, and he was sure the resulting image would attract attention. Since he regarded the job as a forgery rather than a start-from-scratch painting, Lane called in a highly skilled retoucher, Howard Carriker, to produce the art. Using a reproduction of the original as an exact guide, Carriker, who had never worked as an illustrator before, copied David's work meticulously in every detail but four. Marat's dead face has been replaced by Goodman's smiling portrait. No trace of blood remains on the linen drapery. The note in

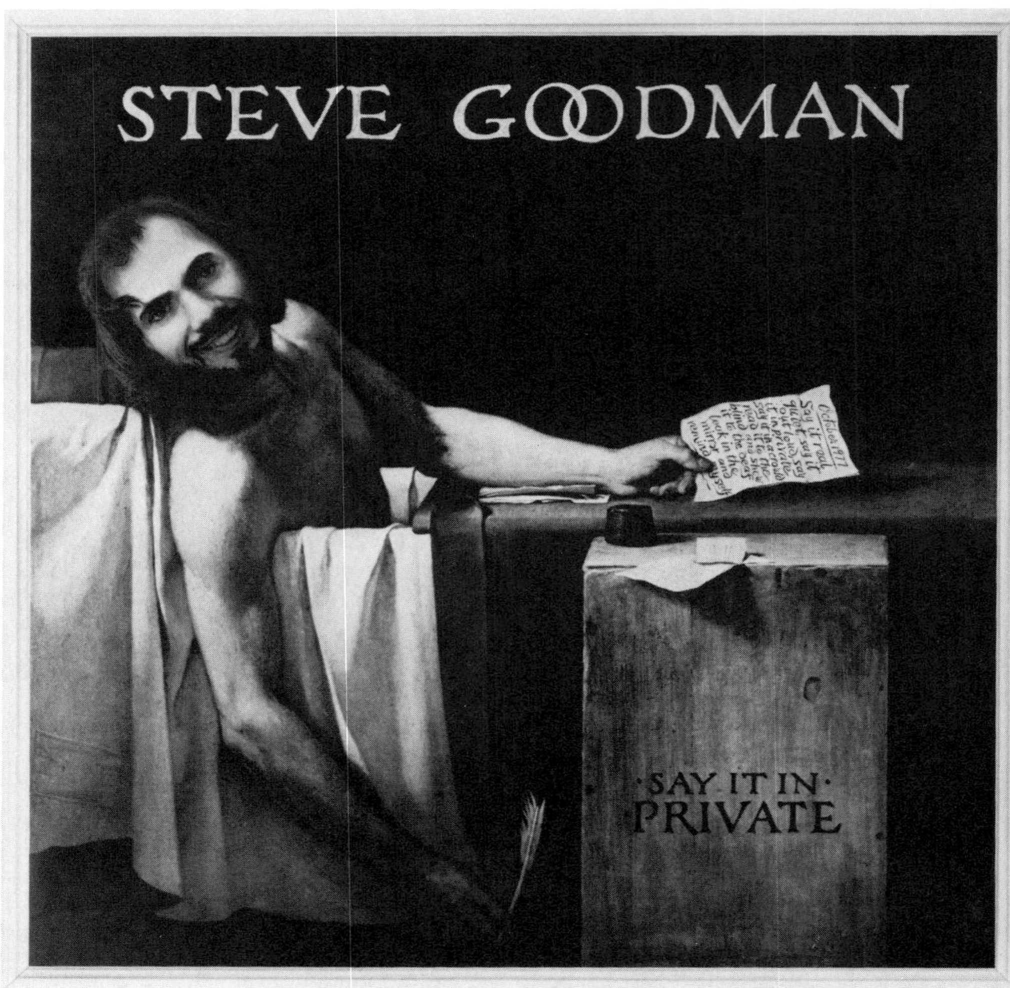

Goodman's hand contains lyrics from the title song; and David's signature with the dedication "À Marat" has been painted out to allow room for the album's title. Michael Manoogian did the lettering directly on Carriker's art. The back cover, however, is even more inspired. Carriker's precise scene is shown again, but alas, the bathtub is empty. Goodman has disappeared in search of drier surroundings. Or perhaps he has gone to vocalize in the shower.

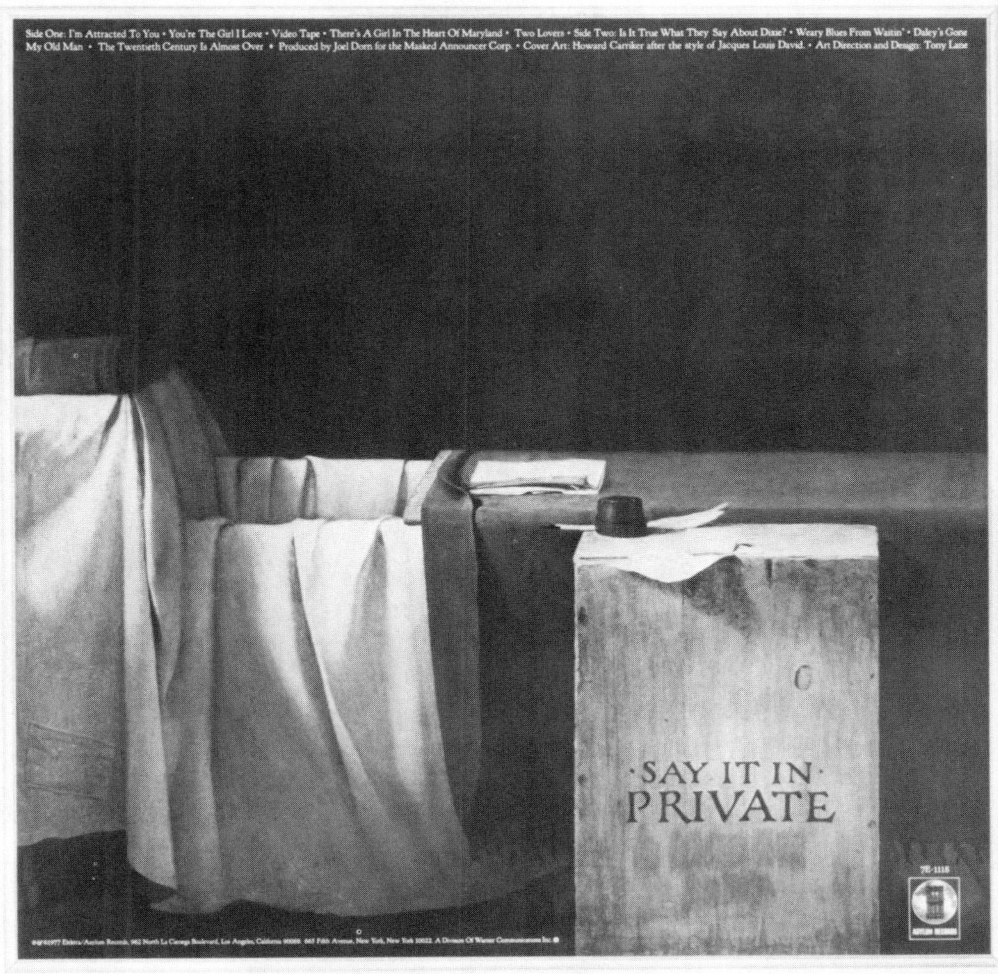

Client: Elektra/Asylum Records
Art director/designer: Tony Lane
Copywriter: Steve Goodman
Illustrator: Howard Carriker
Letterer: Michael Manoogian

The Tolkien Companion

Joseph Zucker first started reading Tolkien's stories when he was a student at Parsons. For his own personal enjoyment he began doodling at random, making sketches of the most interesting characters and episodes. It wasn't long before these illustrations had joined forces to become a Tolkien portfolio which Zucker took to Ian Summers at Ballantine Books in the hope of illustrating a Tolkien calendar. To Zucker's dismay, that job had already been commissioned, but Summers liked the work and having heard about the *Tolkien Companion* project via the grapevine, sent him off to Paul De Angelis at St. Martin's Press. It was a fortuitous meeting. Zucker was asked to do a wrap-around cover illustration which could be used on both the St. Martin's hardback version of the *Tolkien Companion* and Avon Books' paperback edition. Under the direction of Riva Danzig at St. Martin's and Barbara Bertoli at Avon, Zucker, who was asked to recreate the spirit of the stories rather than any one particular scene, conjured up the root-trammeled mountainous landscape of Middle Earth. Gandalf and two of the dwarfs pursue a seemingly endless journey through the rocky wilderness. For Zucker, it was like being paid for working on a hobby. His only technical problems were centering the characters for two different sizes and adding enough edge to the wash/watercolor/pen-and-ink drawing to allow for bleed. Unfortunately, the garish metallic red ink of the title detracts from the quiet moodiness of Zucker's painting.

But the story doesn't end here. At this writing, Zucker has pulled up stakes and moved to Los Angeles where he is drawing his beloved Tolkien characters over and over for Ralph Bakshi's forthcoming animated film version of *The Lord of the Rings*.

Publishers: St. Martin's Press, Avon Books
Art directors: Riva Danzig, Barbara Bertoli
Illustrator: Joseph Zucker
Typography: Pan Books Ltd. (front cover), Larry Hobson (back cover)

The Girl in the Hairy Paw

King Kong has become America's most beloved mythical beast. The creature everyone loves to be afraid of is riding high on a wave of nostalgia, and so far no one has invented a pet monster to replace him. Jaws is only dangerous to swimmers. King Kong could turn up anywhere.

Taking advantage of Kong's popularity, Avon Books decided to publish a documentary study of the making of the original *King Kong*. For less than obvious reasons, the rights to this highly marketable package specifically forbade the use of the monster's name in the title. The editors met the challenge with a fetching substitute, *The Girl in the Hairy Paw*, but they agreed that the cover art must indicate beyond a shadow of a doubt that the book was about King Kong. Illustrator Dave Willardson was supplied with a generous selection of the stills to be reproduced inside and asked to create a cover that would identify the paperback as a book about the making of a movie. Willardson's first painting was an original facsimile of an old movie poster advertising the famous film. "I painted it with tattered edges, in a cockeyed position as if it were plastered on a wall," he recalls, "but it was rejected because they wanted something that depicted the *making* of the movie." The front of Willardson's final wrap-around version shows King Kong in what might have been a scene from the original movie. Opened flat, the cover reveals a cameraman and a carefully researched 1930s camera focussing on Willardson's recreation. Avon reports that the book has sold well and is now in its second printing.

Client: Avon Books
Art director: Barbara Bertoli
Designer/illustrator: Dave Willardson

Above: Willardson's first cover idea, a facsimile of a 1930s movie poster.

Art Kane

A printer in search of a photographer, Bob Ott, president of the Hennegan Company, approached Art Kane with an attractive suggestion. If Kane agreed, Ott wanted to publish a portfolio of his work as a Hennegan promotion piece. It would be a mutually beneficial venture. Kane could enjoy a superbly printed showcase of some of his best photography, and Hennegan would have a distinguished vehicle with which to demonstrate its lithography skills. Neither time schedule nor budget was a limiting factor.

The obvious cover solution was one of Kane's photographs, a shot taken in Brazil in 1977, selected from the available material by Kane and Miho, the designer. "The ultimate effectiveness of this very simple cover solution lies in the choice of the photograph," Miho observes. "It had to suggest Art Kane's unique vision, his talent and his highly developed sense of what makes people stop and look." The printing, rich with subtle contrasts and velvety depths, was straight four-color process with an extra gray for the caption type.

Clients: The Hennegan Co.; Art Kane
Art director/photographer: Art Kane
Designer: Miho

Spreads from Art Kane/Hennegan promotion piece. Top to bottom: Joe Louis, Louis Armstrong (Esquire); The Who, Janice Joplin (Life); Brazil 1977, Bogalusa, Louisiana (Look).

Like the proverbial cleaning lady who doesn't do floors, Malcolm Grear Designers won't do covers *unless* they happen to be designing the rest of the book as well. "We think the book reflects from the inside out—from text, to title page, to half-title, to endpaper, to cover," says Grear, explaining this unusual policy. Producing a cover design that doesn't grow organically from a publication's content makes for too superficial a job, he feels.

Since the firm was doing the entire catalog for an exhibition of Paul Klee's work at the Guggenheim Museum during the summer of 1977, they undertook the graphic resolution of the cover as well. To reflect the broad scope of the artist's *oeuvre*—the wit, candor, and serenity of his approach—without reproducing any one painting, Grear, with designers Bill Newkirk and Pat Rhodes, settled on a simple photogram of a piece of burlap, on which Klee sometimes painted. The colors, a subtle shade of blue on dusty rose, were chosen to reflect Klee's sensitive palette and printed with Newkirk's supervision. The title, a 90 per cent hand-drawn outline reworked from a Gothic typeface, was planned to keep the design open and recall the spatial/linear quality of the artist's pictures. In trying to capture the spirit of Klee's work, the designers have produced a cover that seems authentically 1920s.

Client: Solomon R. Guggenheim Museum
Design firm: Malcolm Grear Designers, Providence, RI
Art director: Malcolm Grear
Designers: Bill Newkirk, Pat Rhodes
Letterer: Bill Newkirk

Weegee

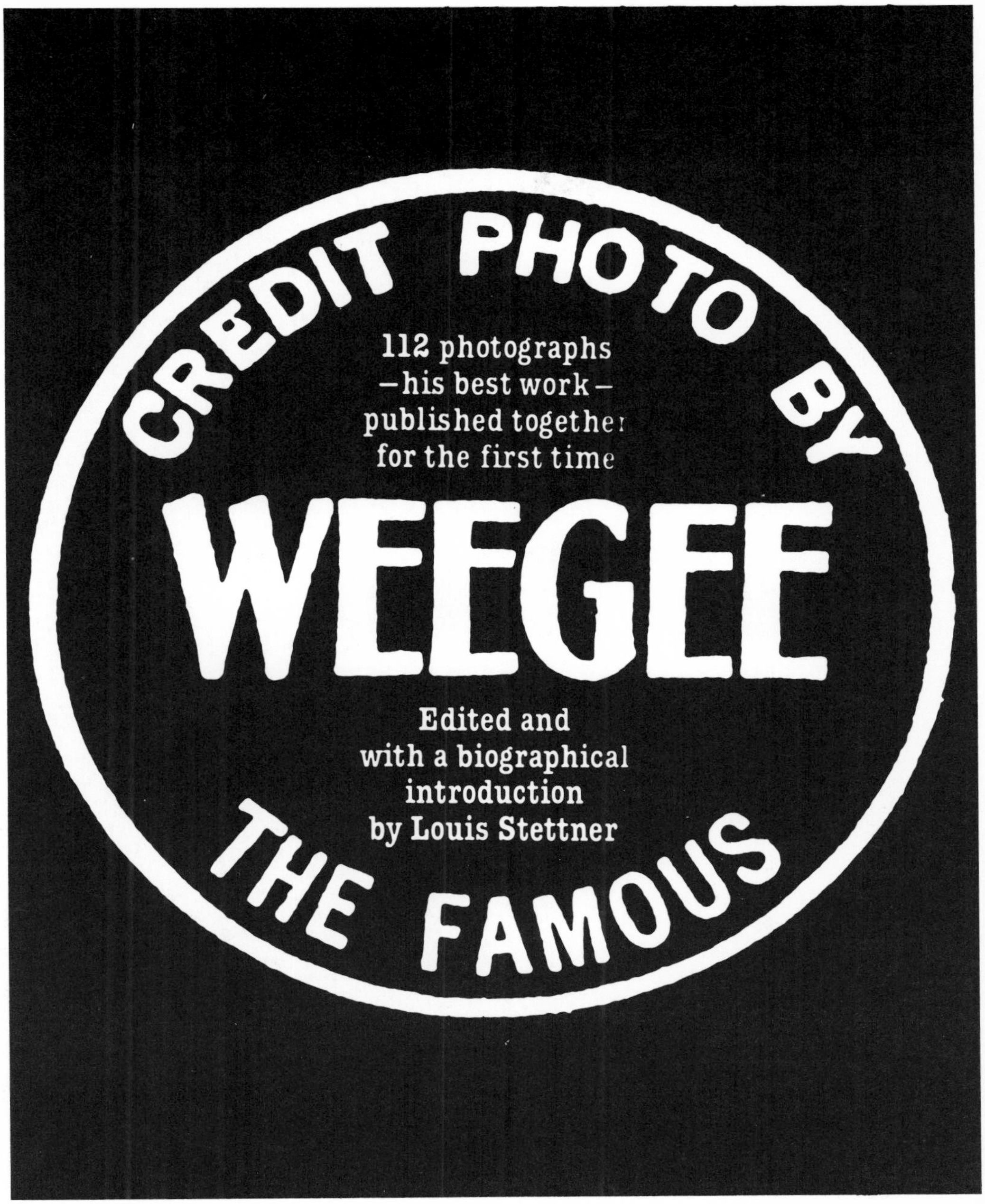

Weegee (Arthur Fellig), a New York-Lower-East-Side-kid-turned-darkroom-technician-and-finally-news-photographer, was a tough, talkative reporter who travelled around in a Chevrolet with a police radio and a portable darkroom in the trunk, and he turned photojournalism into art — although as Louis Stettner points out in his introduction to this collection of the photographer's work, "he never consciously understood the esthetic reasons that made some of his photographs great." He was known for his humanity, his humor and his penchant for promoting himself, symbolized by the familiar stamp, "Credit Photo by Weegee, the Famous."

After a brief flirtation with the idea of using one of Weegee's photographs on the cover of Stettner's book, the editor, and designer Lidia Ferrara, decided that the stamp would make a more comprehensive and dramatic graphic image. A photograph of Weegee and his mobile lab could be shown on the jacket's back. Even with the basic design idea settled, there were still problems. Ferrara considered various devices for emphasizing the photographer's seal—complicated production processes such as debossing the circle and the letters in a white metallic ink. In the end, the simplest presentation proved the most effective—a reverse linecut in black-and-white.

Publisher: Alfred A. Knopf, Inc.
Art director/designer: Lidia Ferrara

CREDIT PHOTO BY

112 photographs
—his best work—
published together
for the first time

WEEGEE

Edited and
with a biographical
introduction
by Louis Stettner

THE FAMOUS

New Jersey, America's Main Road

John Cunningham's popular history of New Jersey had already been published in hardback when Richard Mantel was asked to design the cover of a paperbound edition. The kaleidoscopic one-volume survey called for a comprehensive illustration depicting not only the general nature of the physical landscape but also specific historic personalities who had figured prominently in New Jersey's past. Mantel's first step was to read the text and pick out the characters and events that seemed the most interesting from a visual point of view. With a six-week schedule for sketch and finished art, and no budget for picture research, he stormed the files of the New York Public Library picture collection in search of all the appropriate bits and pieces. Putting them together was a challenge. As a stage for his anachronistic assemblage, Mantel resorted to a typical turn-of-the-century device and painted an elaborate architectural frame. His troop of players were reduced to the same scale, hand-tinted and fixed in position. Prints of a rural landscape and Newark, the typical Garden State city, were dropped into specially cut windows. Only the two Indians and Woodrow Wilson's face had to be conjured up from Mantel's imagination. The final collage was a straight four-color printing job with the type dropped in on an overlay.

Publisher: Doubleday & Co., Inc.
Art director: Alex Gotfryd
Designer: Richard Mantel

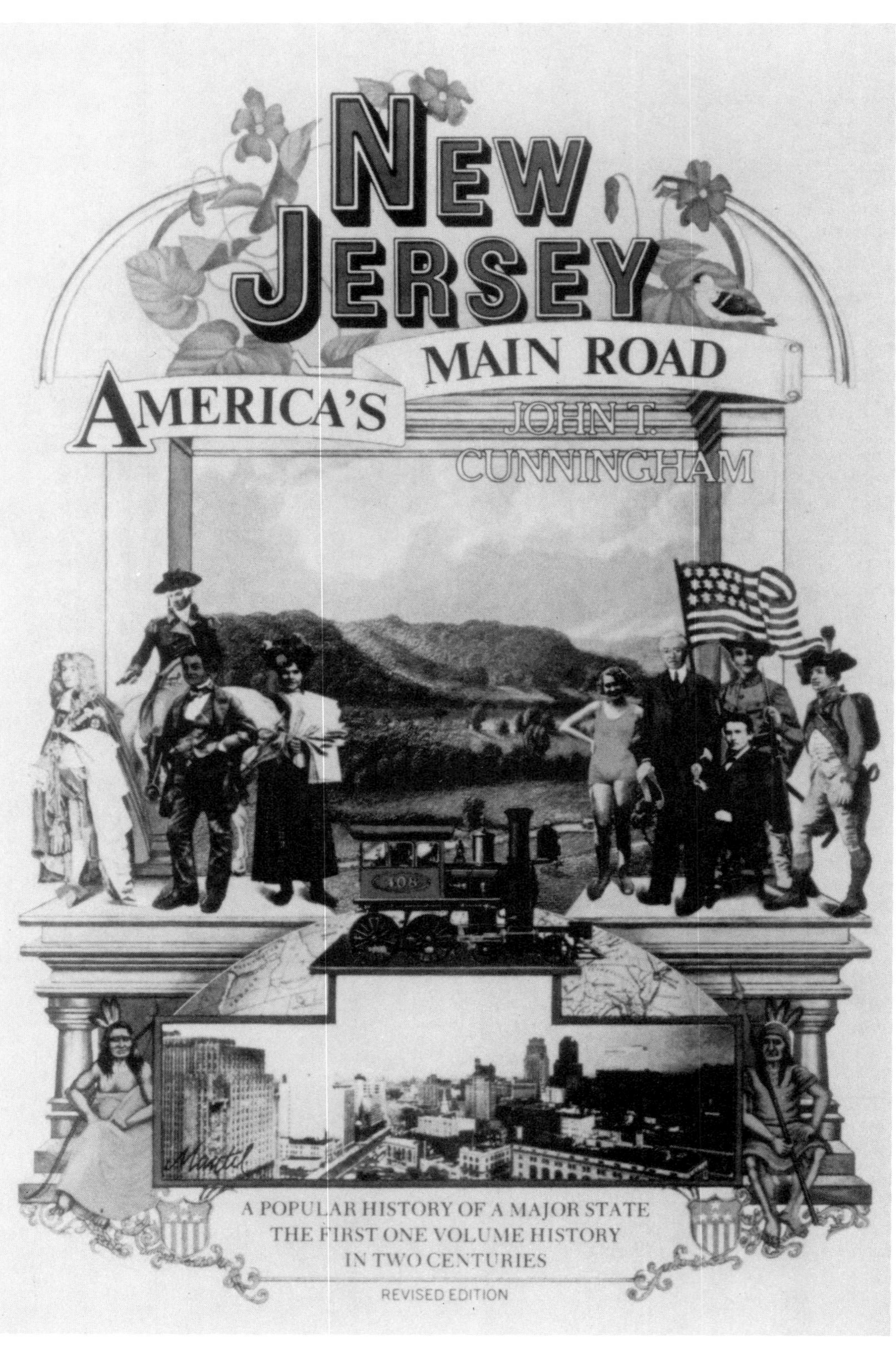

Uncle Sam up to his knees in water and bath toys makes an offbeat, humorous cover illustration for Time, the ordinarily serious weekly news magazine. Art director Walter Bernard planned the cover to function as a small poster which would invite potential readers to investigate the feature story on the Panama Canal Treaty. He sketched the idea and asked Wilson McLean, whose sense of humor and feeling for surrealism seemed appropriate, to do the painting. "It was fun to do," McLean recalls; "it wasn't the typical Time cover portrait and I liked the idea of doing something different." Basing his illustration on Bernard's rough layout, photographs of the canal, 1930s-style drawings of Uncle Sam, and some pictures of boats, McLean submitted two comps—a front view and an aerial, three-quarters side view with the canal running as a band from left to right. "I preferred the second comp because it was a more graphic idea," the artist remarks, "but the head-on pose was the one which they accepted."

Unusually high newsstand sales for the issue indicate that this kind of humorous attack on an unsuspecting public may be an approach for Time to follow more often.

Publisher: Time Inc.
Art director/designer: Walter Bernard
Illustrator: Wilson McLean
Copywriter: Henry Grunwald

Fantasy Records

Reckless Abandon

Album covers can swing in a number of different directions depending on the circumstances. The design inspiration doesn't necessarily come from the music. The wacky comics on a recent Dave Bromberg release, for example, stem from the performing artist's feeling for a turn of phrase and his friendship with cartoonist B. Kliban. Bromberg had seen a strip of crazy Kliban drawings called "The Italian Art of Self-Defense" and, with art director Phil Carroll's concurrence, asked Kliban to come up with the same kind of zany display for his new album. The strongest cut in the album was a song called "What a Town" and two of the roughs featured alligators and other assorted out-of-place creatures hanging out on an urban street. However, Bromberg, who had named a previous album *How Late'll Ya' Play Till* (the verbatim query of a Long Island concert-goer), has an ear for a catchy title. The third rough took off from the words "reckless abandon," which appealed to Bromberg as the *mot juste* for audience reaction to his music. The ridiculous ecstasies of Kliban's dancers provide a perfect label for Bromberg's good-natured rhythms.

There was no doubt at all about the peg on which to hang the album design for Bill Summers' *Feel the Heat.* Summers' music is salsa-jazz based on a mixture of African, West Indian and Latin rhythms. He calls his band Summers Heat and designer Lance Anderson knew that the

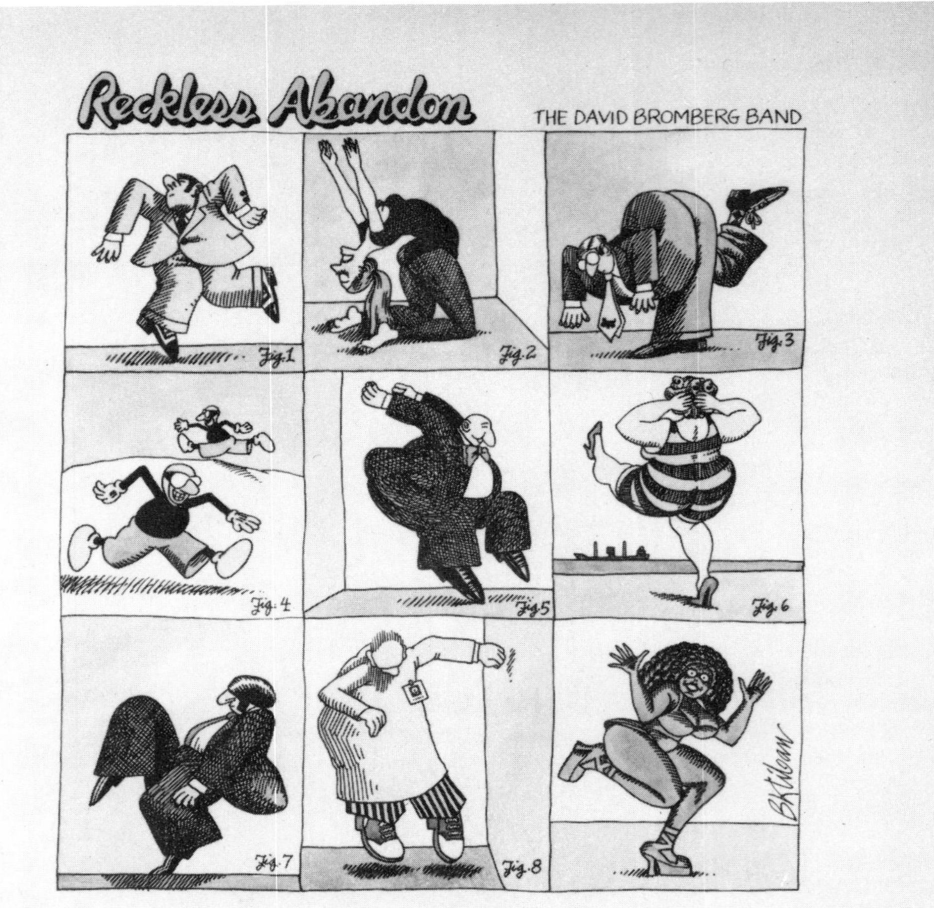

Client: Fantasy Records
Art director: Phil Carroll
Illustrator/designer: B. Kliban

motif had to summon up the sultry atmosphere of tropical surroundings. In compliance with Summers' request that the art suggest the exotic equatorial origins of his music, Anderson asked Jamie Putnam to paint seven miniature travel posters, colorful and geographically descriptive but simple enough to serve as a backdrop for the letters of Summers' name. The background was originally planned as a simple flat color. "But," recalls Carroll, "we all realized at a certain point that it needed something." Carroll's airbrushed red and yellow sweat drops more than solved the problem. Indeed, they have become the tail that wags the dog.

Client: Prestige Records
Art director: Phil Carroll
Designer: Lance Anderson
Illustrators: Jamie Putnam, Phil Carroll

Mr. Flute

Art Webb is a jazz flutist; because his instrumental album, *Mr. Flute*, had a distinct disco flavor, Lynn Breslin, of Atlantic Records, thought it would be interesting to forego obviously popular cover graphics in favor of a classical image of Webb as the Greek god Pan, player of reed pipes.

Enlisting the talents of illustrator Mark Hess, Breslin outlined her idea and supplied him with an old engraving of Pan in a wooded setting and some studio shots of Webb playing his flute. From that point on, Hess followed his own scrupulously detailed inimitable road. He based his formal composition on a landscape typical of the 19th-century American painter Edward Hicks. The hooved Webb/Pan figure perches on a rock in front of a leafy background. A gentle river flows away into a bright distant landscape. "The scene is natural and real; various animals hide in the foliage," comments Hess. "Pan is the only unnatural image. The flute itself connects him to the modern world."

Brilliantly conceived and handsome as a work of art in its own right, Hess's painting did not, he reports, sell records. It is difficult to assess just why that should be so. The image is certainly strong enough to attract attention on a rack amid the competition. Could it be that Webb's music is the negative factor?

Client: Atlantic Records
Art directors: Lynn Breslin, Bob Defrin
Illustrator: Mark Hess

Left: Hess' preliminary sketches.

Arts and the Aging

The National Center on the Arts and the Aging, supported in part by a grant from the National Endowment for the Arts, was established in 1973 by the National Council on the Aging to sponsor workshops, seminars and conferences designed to encourage older people to participate in the arts. Late in 1976, following a conference convened to focus attention on the Center's activities, a report on the conference proceedings was put together and published under the title, "Arts and the Aging, an Agenda for Action." Intended primarily for distribution to conference participants, who included poets, actors, painters, craftsmen, musicians, social workers and physicians, the publication was also to be sold through the National Council on the Aging and in some Washington, D.C., bookstores.

With this somewhat loosely organized marketplace and an audience comprised mainly of professional people, designer Ann Chaparos decided that the graphic treatment of the cover should represent the subject matter in a way that readers would find respectful. Working with conference coordinator Jacqueline Sunderland and editor Peter Smith on a schedule that allowed only three weeks from first editing of the manuscript to delivery by the printer, Chaparos hit upon an idea as simple as it is effective. She chose as an image an illustration from her own collection of advertising postcards dating from the late 1800s. It was originally a mailer touting the benefits of Burdick's Blood Bitters, a kind of 19th-century Geritol guaranteed to rejuvenate consumers. Chaparos simply retouched the original, deleting from the peeled corners of the portrait the name of the old-fashioned tonic. The new version was printed as a black/gray duotone with the peeled corners in a warm red, symbolizing the regeneration of the spirit if not the body.

Chaparos is quite satisfied with the outcome of the project. The final art worked well as an expression of an important quote on the inside cover by John A. B. McLeish* and the printer did an excellent job of reproducing the illustration.

Publisher: National Council on the Aging
Art director/designer: Ann Chaparos

*"... creativity cannot be taught and learned as one can teach and learn a language—but certain conditions, *all of them potentially available in the later years*, can be fostered so that the creative attitude and powers, on whatever scale, can be liberated.

The most important of these conditions are maintenance of a sense of wonder toward life, openness to experience, the sense of search, and scope for the best of the child-self which is present in all of us."

The Artistic Animal

This inquiry into the biological roots of art puts forward the premise that man's esthetic aptitude can be traced to his animal ancestors. According to designer Richard Mantel, the theory that art is not the special province of the human species is not new. *The Artistic Animal,* however, is better documented than other studies have been and, as a result, the theory is gaining credence.

When Mantel was asked to design the cover of this Doubleday paperback, he didn't have a clearly formulated idea of what to do. His problem was unusual—to make a credible, serious presentation of subject matter which might be considered silly. With the vague notion that his sketch should include the image of a chimpanzee, an animal which had figured prominently in experiments discussed in the text, Mantel decided to scour the monkey file in the New York Public Library picture collection for inspiration. "I wanted to find something visual that would give me a way to integrate anthropology and art," he recalls. Scores of pictures later, Mantel noticed one small head that suggested to him the shape of a dollop of paint on an artist's palette. It was the key to his solution. The tiny silhouette prompts a visual double-take that parallels the double-take called forth by the text. As Mantel explains, "Within our normal creative spectrum there is something that we don't see at first, something we have to add to our concept of our creative selves."

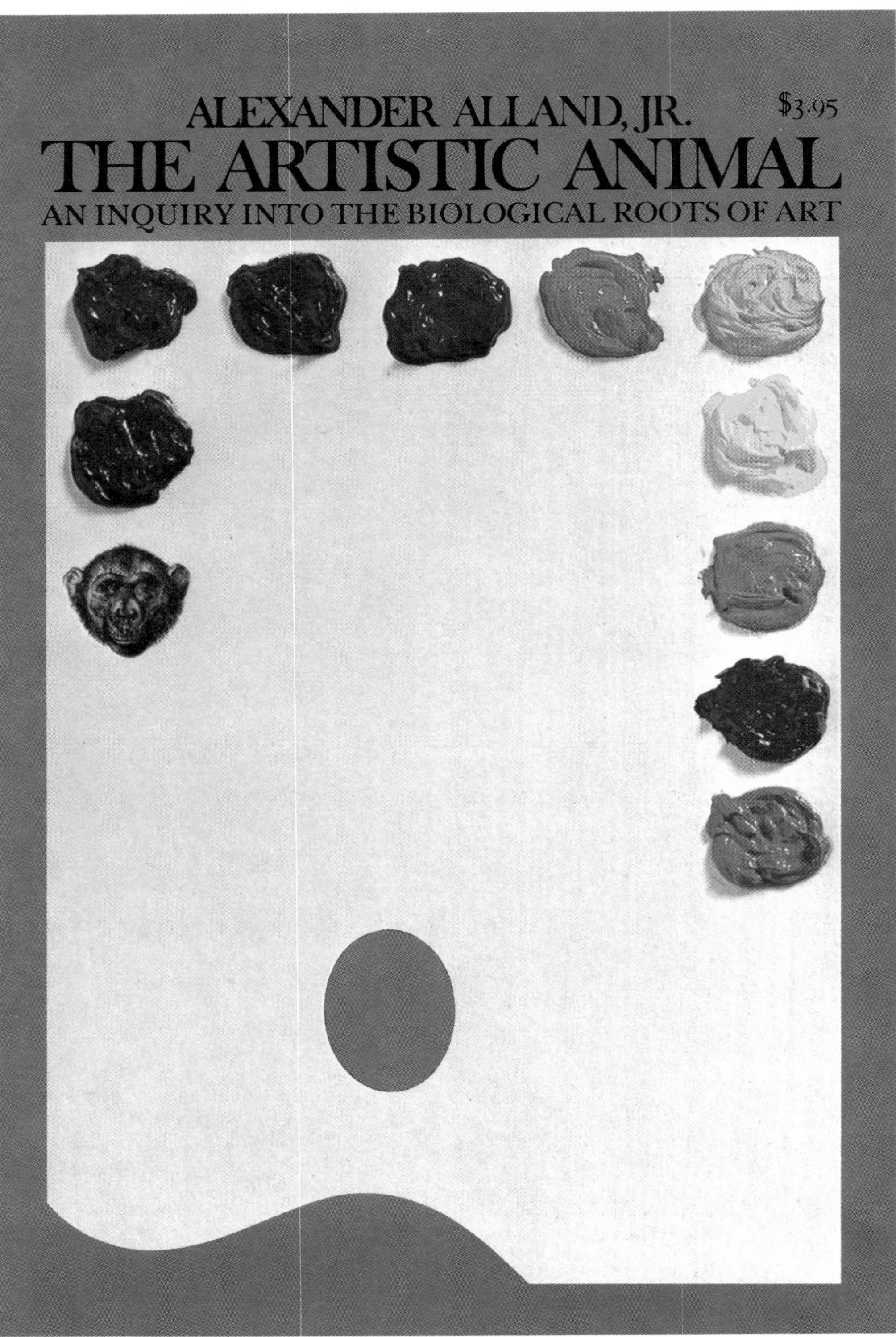

Publisher: Doubleday & Co., Inc.
Art director: Diana Klemin
Designer: Richard Mantel
Photographer: Don Hunstein

A Family Album

A Family Album deals with the ambiguities of perception. A novel of reminiscence covering an extended period of time, the book examines the subtle differences between the reality of a remembered episode, the reality of a photographed moment, and the truth itself. "The book explores what photographs and our memories do to reality," explains designer Richard Mantel: "they are all true and they all lie."

Using a nostalgic old photograph furnished by art director Harris Lewine, Mantel repeated it, enlarged it, reduced it and cut it apart into a regular pattern of grid-like rectangles. The resulting collage moves forward, recedes, and seems to flicker like a silent movie. It is an image which accurately suggests the various levels of reality, both past and present, considered in the text.

A FAMILY ALBUM
A NOVEL
DAVID GALLOWAY

Publisher: Harcourt Brace Jovanovich
Art director: Harris Lewine
Design firm: Push Pin Studios, New York
Designer: Richard Mantel

Print

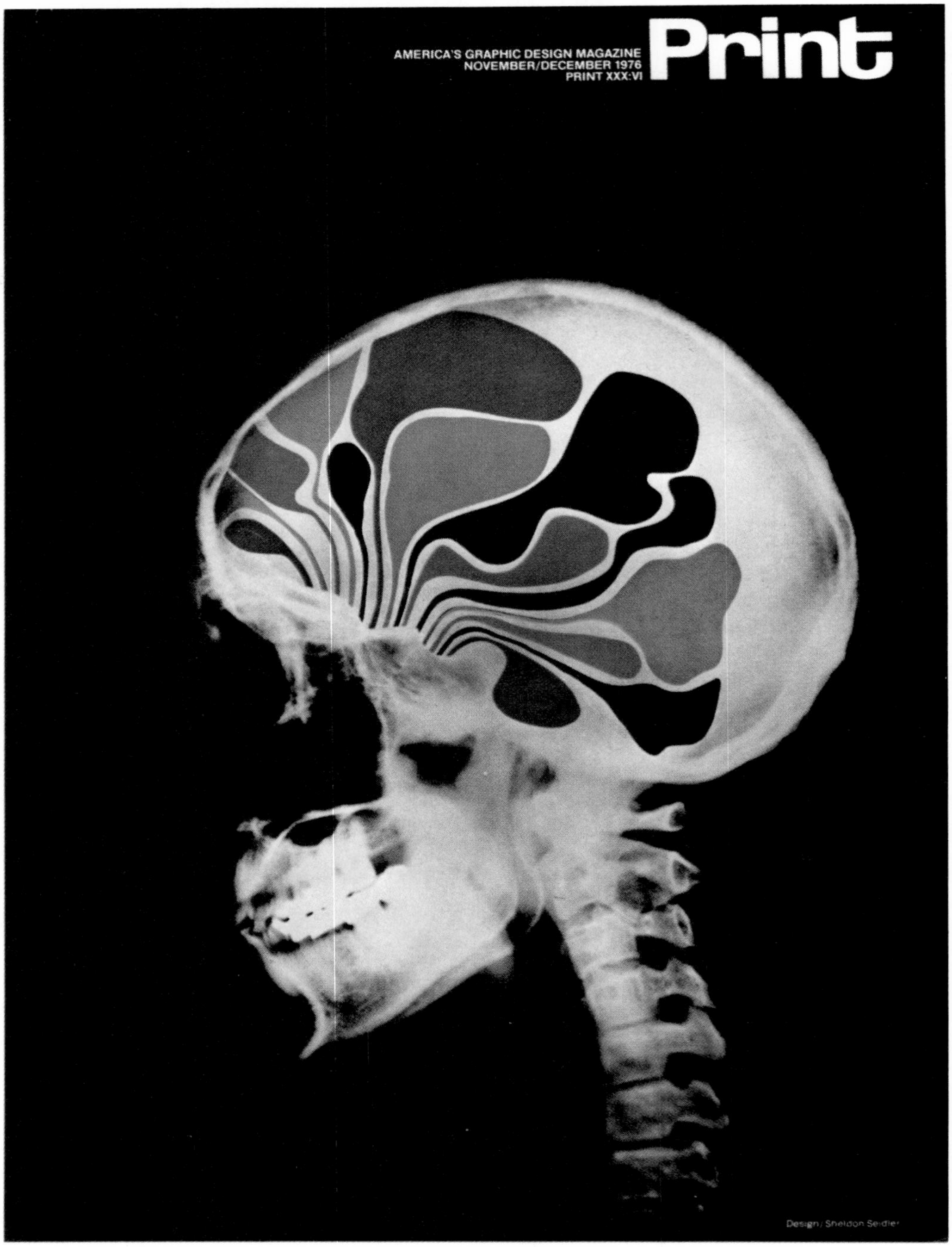

When Sheldon Seidler was asked to design the cover of an issue of PRINT magazine, which featured a portfolio of his work, his first idea was to do a portrait of the prototypical designer. As he turned the concept over in his mind, however, he decided it would be more interesting to present a cross section of a designer's thought processes with a cervical X-ray. Using himself as model, Seidler made an appointment with a radiologist who tried to dissuade him with a dramatic description of the damaging effects of radiation. Seidler won the argument, but his troubles were not over. The radiologist was skilled at skeletal photography, but getting the right exposure for a shot that would include both Seidler's skull and a shadowy profile of his face was tricky business. It took four separate exposures and a good half hour of posing. The result was successful, however, and it only remained for Seidler to retouch the black background slightly and strip in the colored brains.

PRINT's art director, Andrew Kner, whose role in relation to portfolio-generated cover designs is peripheral, limited more or less to giving advice about technical problems, sees in Seidler's design a similarity to previous PRINT covers. "Several designers in the past have come up with variations on the theme that design is happening inside the designer's head," Kner remarks. "Unfortunately, many businessmen we work with don't understand this. They tend to consider design as nothing more than a technical skill. As a result, when designers try to explain design, they often feel compelled to explain it as a cerebral process which involves the intellect."

Two earlier PRINT covers which similarly describe the creative process as a function of the intellect. Right: illustration by Isadore Seltzer; far right: illustration by Barbara Bascove.

Publisher: RC Publications, Inc.
Art director: Andrew P. Kner
Designer: Sheldon Seidler

The Widower's Son

The Widower's Son is a novel by Alan Sillitoe, author of *Saturday Night and Sunday Morning* and *The Loneliness of the Long-Distance Runner*. Like Sillitoe's previous books, it deals with conflicts between background and prospect, class and rank, passion and duty. The visual interpretation of such large concepts requires a sympathetic understanding of the author's point-of-view, and with the concurrence of the British publisher, Sillitoe asked his old friend Leonard Baskin to design the cover. Baskin's pen, ink and wash drawing depicts the central character, a military man whose intimate relationships are infinitely more difficult for him than the rugged discipline of an army career.

When the book was published in the U.S. by Harper & Row, art director Joseph Montebello was given the choice of using the British jacket or commissioning new art. Montebello found Baskin's illustration appropriate and effective, but it required one change for the American edition. In England, only Sillitoe's last name had been used on the cover. Since Baskin's original picture could not be tampered with, Montebello had a new panel made to include the author's full name. Dropped into the space above the military visor, it blends perfectly with the original art.

Publisher: Harper & Row
Art director: Joseph Montebello
Illustrator/letterer: Leonard Baskin

Industrial Launderer

Industrial Launderer is a trade magazine circulated by subscription only to the management of uniform-rental and other cleaning-service companies. One would hardly expect the audience for such a publication to be a visually sophisticated group, but art director Jack Lefkowitz treats them as if they were. Rather than design for the lowest common denominator, he consistently sets his sights high in the expectation that IL's readers will rise to the challenge. No one seems to be complaining and although this year's Casebook jurors selected only two IL covers as winners, there were at least a dozen other deserving Lefkowitz entries.

Without newsstand display or headline copy to rely on as selling tools, Lefkowitz stimulates reader attention with graphics and color. In general, the cover art is inspired by an issue's feature article and Lefkowitz begins work by reading the manuscript and discussing his ideas with editor Jack Roberts. Although his designs always seem spontaneous and appropriate, there are times when the editorial material defies imaginative graphic solution. The lead story for the February 1977 issue, for example, was about the Purity Uniform Service Company. Titled "Purity Profits from Progressive People Policies," it seemed at first to offer no consistent theme on which to base an illustration. "There wasn't much to say about this company," Lefkowitz recalls; "all I could make out about them was that the

management cares about its employees and doesn't hold back on praise and other incentives to keep up the level of production." The mouth offering compliments and roses works well, although Lefkowitz feels, in retrospect, that given the time (it was a rush job) he would have liked to develop it further.

An article in the June 1977 issue offered more promising possibilities. It seems that most industrial cleaning services own fleets of delivery trucks but find it prohibitively expensive to paint them all alike with the same corporate image. IL's June feature described a new process utilizing pressure-sensitive marking film—in laymen's terms, an enormous decal—for truck graphics. Preprinted in large quantities, they can be affixed to both sides of every van in the garage, converting the entire fleet into a team of moving billboards.

Lefkowitz's wife, Pam, works with him as co-designer/illustrator on most IL covers. Her meticulously pre-separated art allows them the advantages of four-color printing without the expense of camera separations. In this case, it must have been a complicated job. Green, turquoise, orange, and magenta flying transfers show off their yellow adhesive undersides against a gray factory background.

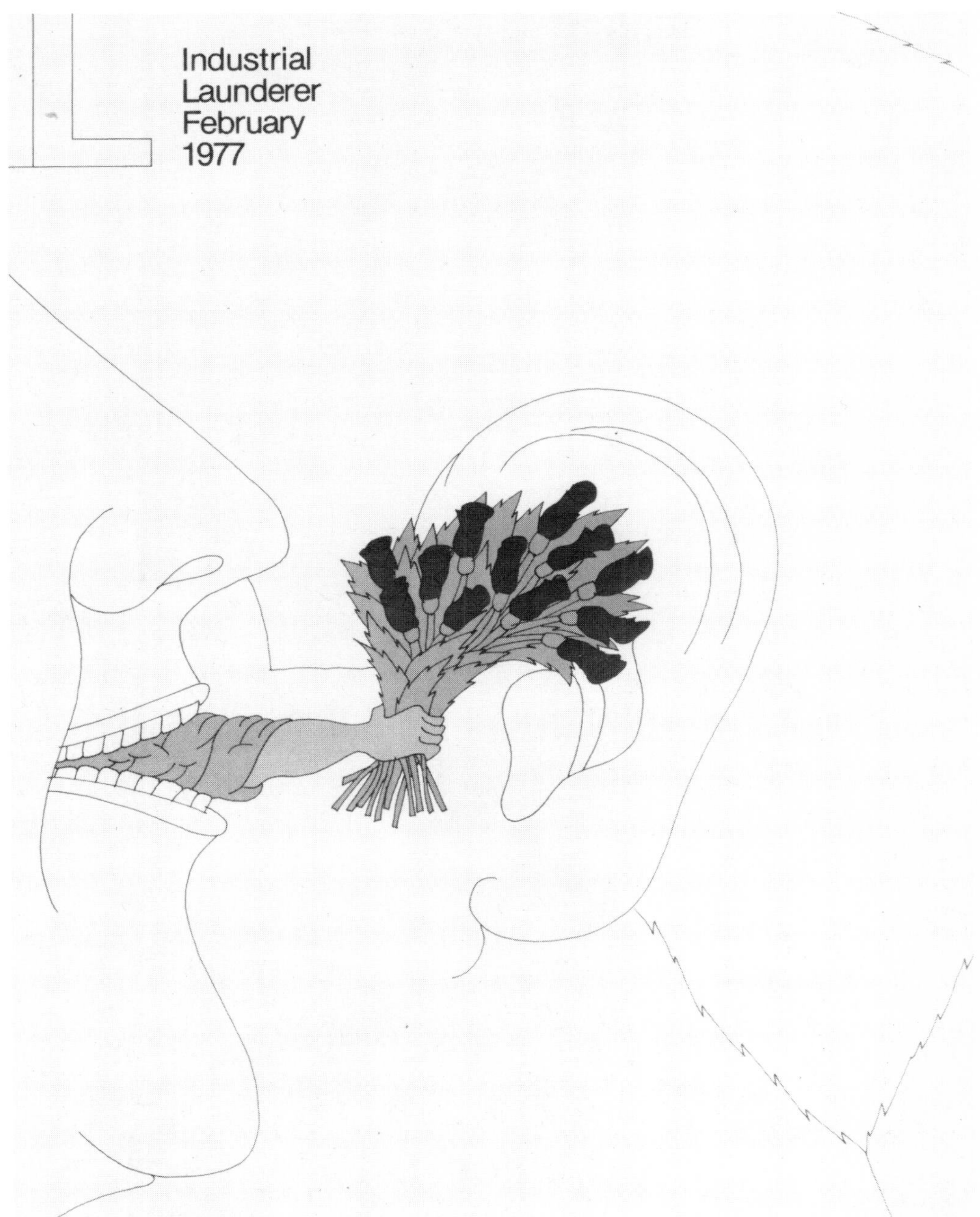

Publisher: Institute of Industrial Launderers
Art director: Jack Lefkowitz
Designers/illustrators: Jack Lefkowitz, Pam Lefkowitz

Parties

Carl Van Vechten was an American music critic, photographer and novelist whose evocative portrait of the Roaring Twenties was painted in a series of seven novels over a period of approximately ten years. When Avon Books decided to reissue *Parties* in a paperback edition, they wanted a cover illustration which would recall the glittering dissipation of a society on the brink of economic disaster. "We asked an English artist, Graham Percy, to do the painting," says designer Don Munson, "because his style was nostalgic but fresh, and we knew he could evoke the plastic elegance of the demimonde on a high which wouldn't last long." Avon's choice of illustrator was almost too perfect. Percy's first sketch came in looking too much like the real thing, an authentic '20s book jacket. The revised version, stylized somewhat to give it a more contemporary impact, was published as a literary piece in the Avon Bard format, a signal to bookstore personnel that the novel is a sophisticated work which should appeal to the intelligentsia.

Left: detail of cover illustration incorporated into Avon's Bard trademark for use on back cover.

Publisher: Avon Books
Art director: Barbara Bertoli
Designer: Don Munson
Illustrator: Graham Percy

Brassai: The Secret Paris of the 30's

Perhaps because he was an Eastern European, born Gyula Halász in the Hungarian district of Romania, Brassai was able to photograph the underside of Paris with an objective honesty which might not have come so easily to a French photographer. *The Secret Paris of the 30's* documents with humor and sympathy a sordid, tantalizing Parisian low-life which, though common knowledge, was officially proscribed. The pictures are accompanied by Brassai's charming reminiscences about his visits to this forbidden world of transvestite dance halls, opium dens and "houses of illusion."

The cover photograph, taken in a small Latin Quarter brothel, records a scene which the photographer describes in the text. "At Suzy, a bell went off as the client opened the door, and he found himself in a kind of booth, as though he had gone to vote. The madam appeared with a wide, salacious grin. She would clap her hands and call out, 'Choosing time, ladies!' All the girls who weren't otherwise occupied would remove their dressing gowns, their kimonos, pell-mell, and arrive in the simplest of apparel, whereupon they would form a *tableau vivant*."

By reducing the picture to a small square under a colorful neon canopy, the designer has skillfully managed to suggest the tawdry glitter of an unsavory part of town and the prurience of those who visited it. The viewer seems to regard these ladies of the night through a keyhole. The title, expertly vignetted and printed in primary colors whose shadows bleed into the black background, captures the effect of flickering light.

Publisher: Editions Gallimard/ Pantheon Books
Art director/designer: Massin

Heavy Metal is a new, sophisticated science-fiction magazine featuring futuristic epics, interplanetary Westerns, and absurd fantasy—all of it on a higher plane than the run-of-the-mill Marvel Comics fare. Advertising surveys have revealed its audience to be an elite group of college students and recent graduates in their early 20s, devotees of science fiction and fans of Heavy Metal's French sister publication, Metal Hurlant. For the cover of the first issue, which appeared in April 1977, art director Peter Kleinman decided to identify the new magazine as a mirror of the French publication by using as cover art an illustration originally painted for Metal Hurlant by Philippe Druillet. It depicts two fururistic metal robots in a clashing combat which Kleinman describes as "almost audible." This unusual aural/visual symbol serves two purposes. It calls to mind (and ear) the title of the European magazine which literally translated into English would be "Screaming Metal," and it links the futuristic sci-fi cult with the punk-rock movement whose albums are often illustrated with the same kind of art. Kleinman's logo, a straightforward visual pun which complements the detailed commotion of Druillet's drawing, was printed in gold to celebrate the publication's debut.

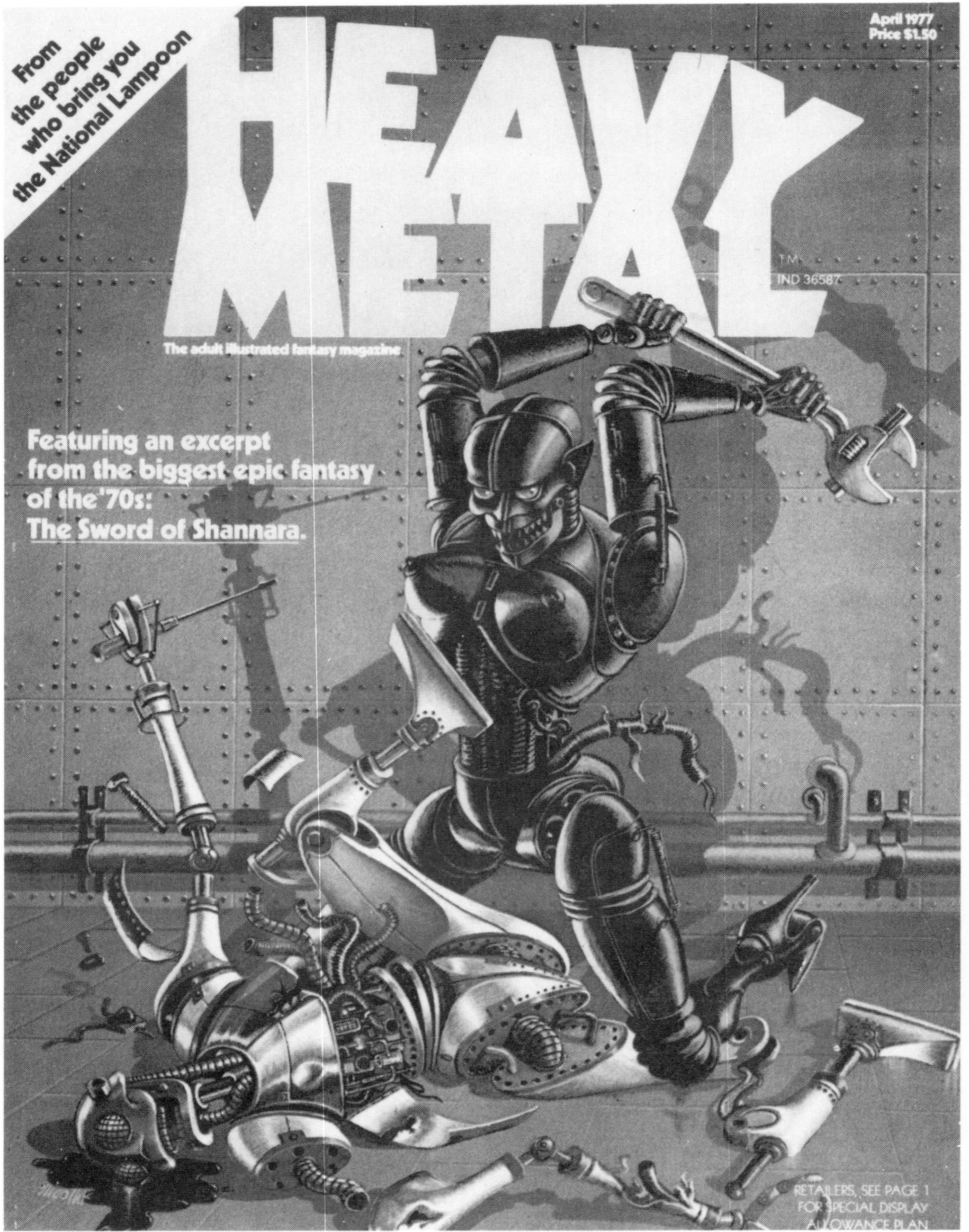

Publisher: Twenty-First Century Communications
Art director/designer: Peter Kleinman
Illustrator: Philippe Druillet
Copywriter: Sean Kelly

Spreads typical of Heavy Metal's editorial content. Top: story by cover artist Druillet; below: story by Marre and Macedo.

Jack: A Biography of Jack London

Designing the book jacket for a biography is a more difficult charge than it seems. The designer hopes to reveal in the limited space allotted to him the essential current and quality of the life inside the book. But reducing the complexities of a personal history to one page of words and pictures is a frustrating task. The words and pictures must be ever so carefully chosen.

When Lawrence Ratzkin was asked to design the cover for Andrew Sinclair's biography of Jack London, the main criterion was to distinguish it clearly from other biographies. Art director Joseph Montebello was quite definite about what to avoid. The solution could be neither all type nor a full-scale picture of the subject. With those specific instructions, he gave Ratzkin two photos of London and left him to his own devices. Ratzkin's solution combines a snapshot of London the seafarer with a thoughtfully chosen typeface. Printed in brown, the photograph seems to have been temporarily borrowed from an old family album. The type is Hogarth, strong, erratic, strung with unsophisticated ornaments, evocative—as Ratzkin planned it to be—of the West and the Klondike gold rush, one of London's turn-of-the-century adventures. Printed in black on a red background, the bold letters portray Jack as a powerful, formidable man.

Publisher: Harper & Row
Art director: Joseph Montebello
Designer: Lawrence Ratzkin

MBA (Master in Business Administration) Magazine is supported by its advertisers and mailed to subscribers free of charge. Its audience of 160,000 readers includes graduate students in their last year of business school and young professionals building their careers. For the January 1977 issue featuring an article titled "Neoconservatives, New Defenders for the Old Order," art director John Jay wanted a cover which would suggest a sense of quiet stability and strength. A gallery show of Roy Carruthers' work convinced him that Carruthers' style was perfect for the topic. "I knew Carruthers was no longer working commercially," Jay recalls, "so I asked if he had an existing work that would be appropriate." Carruthers supplied a painting originally titled "The Psychiatrist," which works equally well as a portrait of a ponderous, wary businessman. His grotesquely foreshortened hand (the symbol of power and ownership?) is even more anatomically abnormal than it seems at first glance. An extra finger, subtly camouflaged by the imperturbable demeanor and apparent impeccability of the figure, gives the cover an added dimension.

Publisher: MBA Communications, Inc.
Art director/designer: John C. Jay
Illustrator: Roy Carruthers

Callahan

Six years ago, Peter Bradford, who has always admired Harry Callahan's photography, extracted a promise from Michael Hoffman of Aperture Books that if and when he published a book on Callahan, Bradford would design it. The project was finally begun in the spring of 1977 so that publication would coincide with a major retrospective exhibition of Callahan's work at the Museum of Modern Art in the fall. The cover design, which took two to three weeks of the entire three-month production schedule, was worked out not on the basis of any practical formula, but intuitively. "Hoffman and the author, John Szarkowski, did not even define their goals," Bradford recalls, "but in talking to them I got a feeling for their sense of Callahan which influenced the work I produced. It was sort of a mutually groping collaboration." The text had described Callahan's pictures as full of grace, antiseptically clean, cold, distant and precise, and it was important to Bradford that the jacket accurately represent the elegance and formality of the work inside. "The approach was so simple that I could afford to experiment extensively with color and texture," says Bradford, who made five different press-on lettering renditions of the one-word title to determine which would best complete the image he had in mind. The photograph of Callahan's wife, one of several possibilities that the publisher and author considered, appealed to Bradford because "it had the character of becoming part of the book." In the final analysis, this cover was an attractive but not unusually complicated design problem. "The biggest contention," says Bradford, "was whether Harry Callahan could be called just Callahan. The design just wasn't a 'Harry' design. If they had insisted on using the full name, I would have had to start all over." Rapoport produced the superb printing Bradford had anticipated.

Publisher: Aperture Books
Art director/designer: Peter Bradford
Photographer: Harry Callahan

CALLAHAN
CALLAHAN
CALLAHAN
CALLAHAN
CALLAHAN

Five preliminary versions of the title.

The Franchiser

The novel behind this cover deals with a man involved in buying franchises. "The pervasive theme," explains Lawrence Ratzkin, who likes to read the manuscript when he is asked to design a book jacket, "is that there is a sameness throughout life, that we are plagued by standardization." His first idea was to suggest both a multiple birth mentioned in the story and the increasingly homogeneous character of our surroundings with the image of a cookie cutter; but that sketch was rejected. "It was one step too removed," notes Ratzkin; "too much interpretation was required." His final solution, a three-color assortment of gasoline-alley highway signs, is direct and to the point.

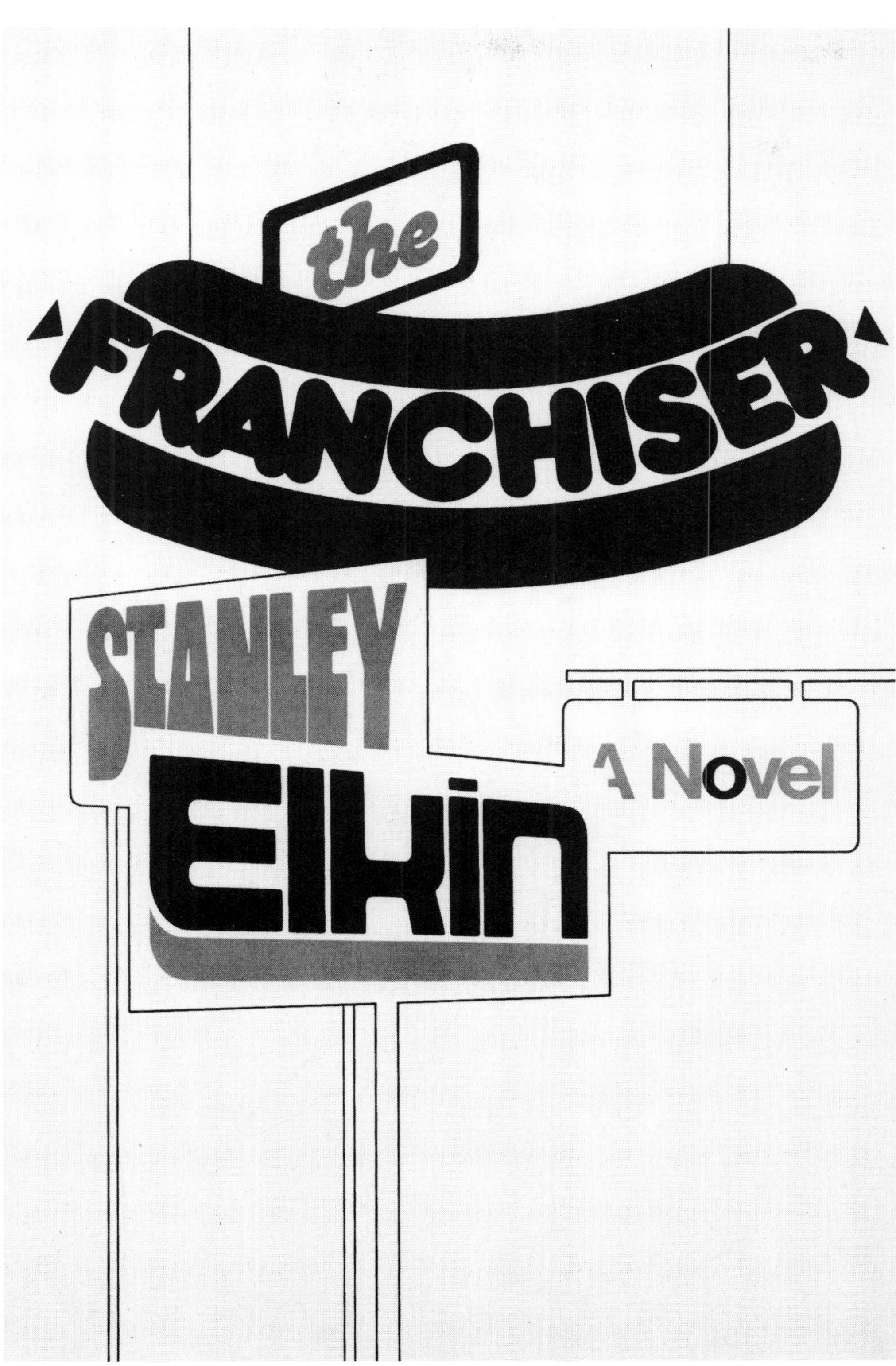

Publisher: Farrar, Straus and Giroux
Art director: Dorris Janowitz
Designer: Lawrence Ratzkin

Fairfield County

The cover story of the July 1977 issue of Fairfield County magazine was about Greenwich, Connecticut, and dealt primarily with the contrast between Greenwich the residential community and Greenwich the haven for corporate headquarters. It also described the town's diverse neighborhoods and attempted to dispel the notion that Greenwich belongs exclusively to the very well-to-do. Although the majority of the publication's previous issues had featured striking four-color illustrations on the cover, the editor decided to break with that tradition in favor of a photograph. "The town of Greenwich (consisting of Byram, Cos Cob, Riverside, Greenwich and Old Greenwich) is fragmented," explains art director Thomas Starr, "and there was no one scene for an illustrator to focus on. While a montage-type illustration could have solved this, it wouldn't have been bold enough for a cover."

Although the publication is circulated by subscription only and Starr was not obliged to design a cover which would promote newsstand sales, he was determined to depict Greenwich's schizophrenic character in one dramatic photograph. Recalling a recently-built mirror-glass office building which reflected older homes in its facade, he knew he had a perfect one-shot picture to illustrate the feature article. "Even if people didn't read the article," says Starr, "I wanted them to understand at a glance what was happening."

Deciding on the subject matter, however, was only half

the battle. Starr's shooting schedule was plagued by overcast and rainy weather. Since the building reflects the sky, a dreary day would make a dreary photograph. Furthermore, the cover was to grace a July issue and Starr wanted bright blue sky with a few fleecy clouds. Like children at the beach on a wet summer weekend, Starr raced outside whenever the rain let up to study the location. As his deadline drew closer, though he still had no usable pictures, he had acquired a thorough understanding of the building, its angle of reflection and its orientation to the sun. When the weather finally cleared, he simply lay down in the middle of the sidewalk and clicked the shutter. "I went to the building at 11 a.m.," he recalls, "when I could count on an evenly bright reflected landscape, a reflected sky that would match and blend with the true sky, and a little glint of sunshine on the chrome window frames." Even the cloud pattern obliged by leaving ample space for the logotype.

Above left: alternate cover photo; above: photographs appearing on opening spread of cover story; left: Starr's preliminary thumbnail sketch.

Publisher: County Communications
Design firm: Thomas Starr & Associates, Greenwich, CT
Art director/designer/ photographer: Thomas Starr
Editor: Elizbeth Hill O'Neil

New York Times Magazine

Jim McMullan's watercolors for a New York magazine article titled "Tribal Rites of the New Saturday Night" have become something of a milestone in the way of contemporary graphics. Not only have they won critical acclaim as a provocative contribution to the new wave of realism in illustration, they are also in all probability the only commercial drawings to have inspired a full-length feature film (*Saturday Night Fever*). On a less public level, they mark an important development in McMullan's personal style—the obsessive use of his own photographic research as a basis for detailed paintings rich with an energy and surface tension totally absent from the original contact prints.

This was the style Ruth Ansel wanted for the cover of a Sunday New York Times Magazine issue featuring an article on the Teamsters union. "Ruth made it clear that she wanted a painting in the spirit of the Brooklyn disco series," McMullan recalls. "She understood that the style had a great deal to do with the staging of the subject matter and was willing to give me a lot of freedom." The editors, however, were initially skeptical. They wanted something dramatic and surreal—trucks coming ominously over the horizon and flying through the air. It was hard for them to understand that the portrait of a truck driver might offer real drama.

To save time in the tight schedule (six days from original commission to final

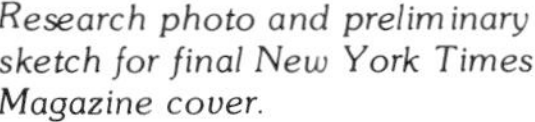

Research photo and preliminary sketch for final New York Times Magazine cover.

art), McMullan based his first sketch on an illustration from a book called *Trucker*. It included the back of a union official requested by Times editors as a symbol of the leadership's control over the drivers. The image was too bland, however, and the editors realized that the addition of a second figure wouldn't work. To produce a weightier, more electric illustration, it was necessary for McMullan to set up his own shot. Using as a model a young contractor with offices directly below his studio, and the cab of a New York Times truck, McMullan got the image he wanted. Ansel suggested substituting the union seal for the union official and the sketch was okayed. For McMullan, the final painting provided the most interesting challenge. "My original colors were more subdued," he recalls. "When Ruth saw the painting, she loved it, but she wanted it darker and brighter. She didn't like the idea of the driver wearing a pink jacket. I worked on it another day and really put on the loud pedal," McMullan continues. "It's probably the darkest, brightest, densest painting I've ever painted."

Publisher: The New York Times
Art director: Ruth Ansel
Illustrator: James McMullan

Top left: research photo from book, "Trucker"; top right: preliminary sketch; above: final, rejected sketch including Teamsters union seal.

In this country, someone can graduate from art school, find a job in the real world, rise through the ranks to become art director of Esquire and then sweat a lot over producing a klutzy matchbook cover that looks as if it wasn't even designed. Given away free with cigarettes, matchbooks flash cheap, unsophisticated advertising geared to a mass market. Esquire, aiming at the same market with a topic of universal interest—"How to Get a Job"—made effective use of the familiar matchbook image. "The idea came from editor Byron Dobell," reports art director Michael Gross, whose previous experience as art director of National Lampoon qualified him as an expert in doing parodies; "all I did was execute it." To make the final cover as authentic as possible, Gross produced an actual-size silk-screened matchbook, devised a layout that would incorporate all the necessary cover lines and got Dick Frank to shoot the photograph. In spite of favorable reaction to the cover and high newsstand sales, Gross was not entirely satisfied with the results. "I thought some reference to the inside of the magazine should have been on the actual matchbook," he explains, "so that it didn't look as if we picked up a real book of matches and simply photographed it." He's right. "A Special 27-Page Survival Guide" would have worked nicely between "JOB" and "Strike on Back Cover."

Another Esquire cover, put together by another art

director, proffers an entirely different treatment. To illustrate the issue's feature presentation, a sequel to James Jones' *From Here to Eternity,* Sam Antupit decided to break an unwritten company rule and commission a painting instead of a photograph. Preliminary conversations with editor Byron Dobell established that the subject matter should relate to Jones' previous war story. "We wanted a version of the old posters but with a more sensitive face," recalls Antupit, who turned the job over to illustrator Richard Hess with a very tight sketch and an assortment of reference material, including an Italian World War II poster and a collection of UPI photos of Guadalcanal. Dobell had originally asked that the soldier's portrait be set against flat red, white and blue stripes, but Hess thought such bold colors would detract from the face and substituted a much dimmer background—the cloth of a battle-weary flag. The final murkiness, however, came as a surprise, Antupit reports; it was the result of inferior printing.

To meet a tight production schedule—five days from original idea to camera deadline—Antupit, using a tracing of the illustration, had the type set and the mechanical begun while Hess was still working on the painting. When the final was delivered, Antupit made a color stat for in-house presentation and sent the art to the engraver. The finished product, which appeared in November 1977, made an

effective contrast with the newsstand competition—a festive array of holiday graphics.

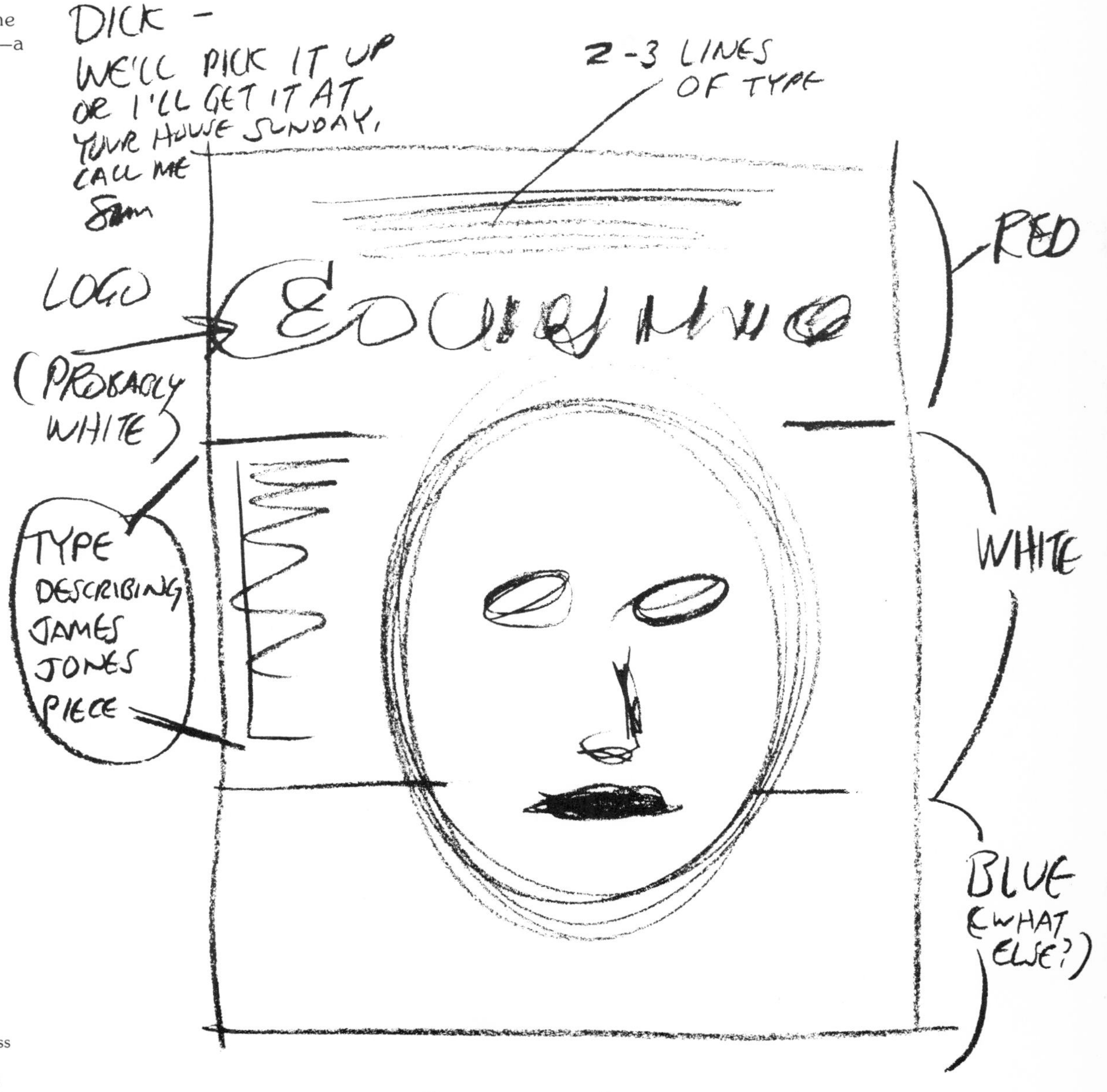

Art director Antupit's sketch for illustrator Richard Hess.

Publisher: Esquire, Inc.
July 1977:
Art director: Michael Gross
Designer: Richard Becker
Copywriter: Byron Dobell
Photographer: Dick Frank
November 1977:
Art director/designer: Sam Antupit
Designer: Richard Becker
Copywriter: Byron Dobell
Illustrator: Richard Hess

New West

New West, like its sister publication, New York, enjoys agitating its audience with occasional crisis covers suggesting that doomsday is just around the corner. Just such an opportunity presented itself during the great Western drought of 1977 with a feature article called "Can We Change the Weather Before It's Too Late?" Art director Lloyd Ziff and designer Steve Hoffman agreed that it would be provocative to show a city like Los Angeles that had turned into an uninhabitable desert. The image reminded Ziff of an alarmingly real photograph that had been made into a poster by Ed Thrasher and John Van Hammersveld a couple of years earlier. Thrasher, seething from the smothering depression of too many smog-alert days, had gone downtown and shot an L.A. street which was nearly indistinguishable owing to the density of the atmospheric conditions. Thrasher sent the resulting poster, titled "Southern California," to every political official in the state, and reports that although he had thought of

"Southern California" poster by Ed Thrasher and John Van Hammersveld which inspired New West cover.

Publisher: NYM Corp.
Art director: Lloyd Ziff
February 28, 1977:
Designer: Steven Hoffman
Illustrator: Joe Heiner

the project as something of a serious lark, the poster won considerable acclaim.

Seeing in Thrasher's photo an image of the prototypical L.A. street, Ziff sent illustrator Joe Heiner out to find the same location and create his desert within its confines. Heiner's wasteland is a photo-collage assembled from various sources and painted here and there so that it is impossible to tell where the photography stops and the illustration begins. Hoffman observes, "It represented a rather dry story in an entertaining way."

In the spring of 1977, Ziff and the editors decided to take advantage of the traditional North/South California rivalry and do a cover suggesting that the state divide in two. The two sections have little in common, not even the weather. Northerners tend to consider the south a hopeless confusion of freeways, gaudy tourist attractions and palm trees, while the southerners see in the north nothing but hippies, conservationists and redwoods. Ziff and illustrator Mick Haggerty decided to portray the argument with a travel poster torn in half to define the two factions. Done in the style of '30s illustrator Joseph Binder, the painting presented only one technical problem: the sky had to be light enough so that different cover lines for the separate northern and southern editions could overprint.

Above left: cover for Southern California edition of New West. It is identical except for cover lines.

May 9, 1977:
Designers: Lloyd Ziff, Mick Haggerty
Illustrator: Mick Haggerty
Copywriter: Frank Lalli

National Lampoon

If Esquire can put out a cover resembling a Lampoon parody (see page 55), then the Lampoon can publish an issue that looks like Time. These are the gimmicks that keep newsstand addicts on their toes. For an edition devoted to an assessment of John F. Kennedy's first 6000 days in office, had he not been assassinated but instead been elected for a third and fourth term, art director Peter Kleinman wanted to make fun of the Kennedy image and mystique without being offensive. He asked Sol Korby, whose Time covers always made the subject look serious and dignified, to do a portrait of JFK as man-of-the-year. Korby based his illustration on the official White House photograph of Kennedy when he took office. Reluctant to make too many radical changes at once, he aged the familiar visage cautiously in a painting which, like the portrait of Dorian Gray, grew old in several stages. In spite of this unaccustomed Lampoon fling with delicacy and good taste (or perhaps because of it), Kleinman reports that the issue did not sell well.

More in keeping with the publication's usually unabashed style is the cover for its July 1977 annual issue about sex. In response to publisher Matty Simmons' dictum, "Put tits on the cover," Kleinman assembled a collection of in-house graffiti. "We were quite rushed," he explains, "so a kid from the mailroom did the drawing and people around the office did the lettering." The various pieces were put together on a

mechanical and shot in line with overlay colors stripped in later by the printer. A four-color photograph of Kleinman's own bathroom tiles provided the background. Attesting to the effectiveness of the cooperative staff effort, this issue was the best-seller of the year. Moreover, Kleinman relates, "Someone in California sued us for using his phone number."

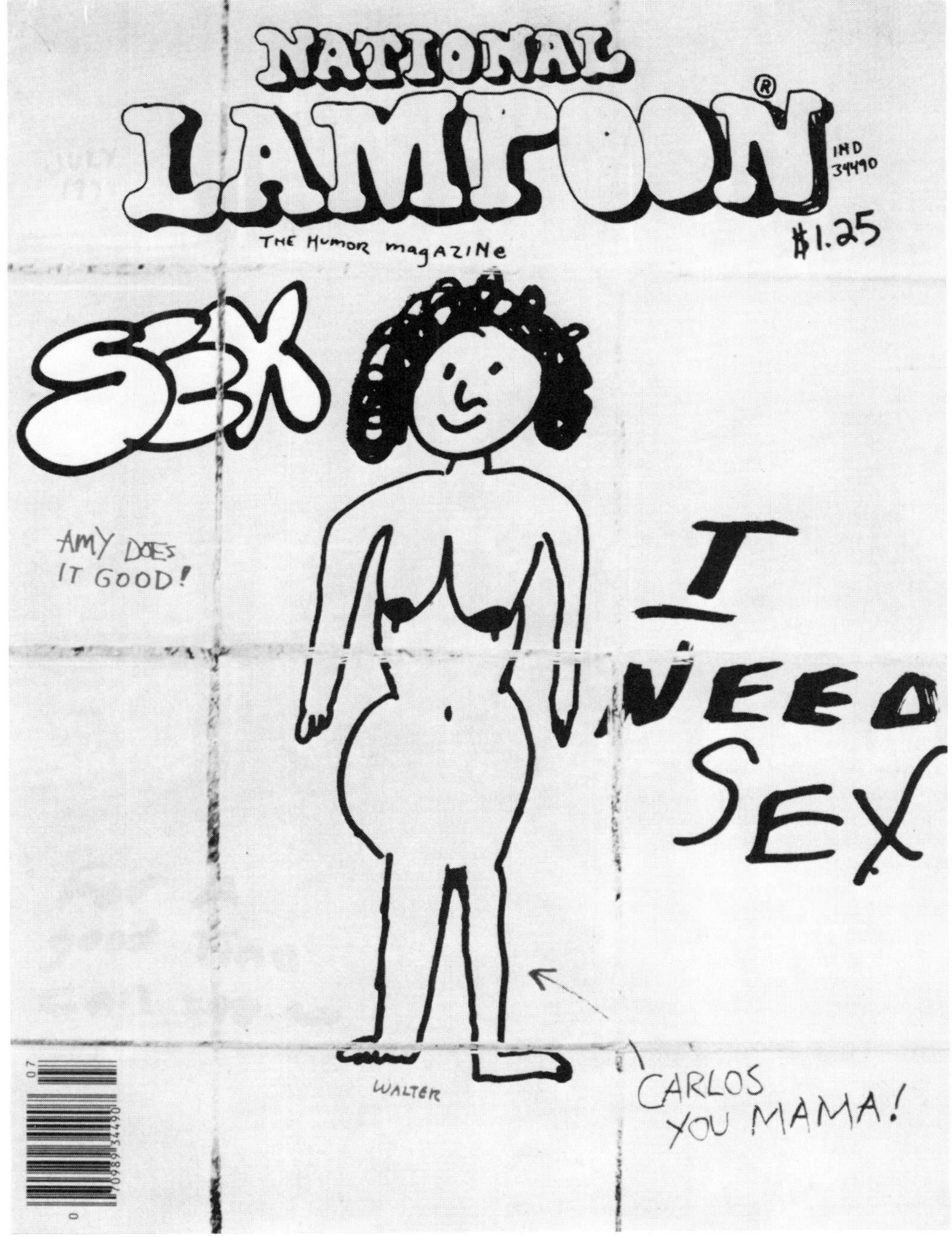

Publisher: Twenty-First Century Communications
Art director: Peter Kleinman
February 1977:
Designer: Skip Johnston
Illustrator: Sol Korby
July 1977:
Illustrator: Walter Garibaldi
Copywriter: Sean Kelly

The Worlds of Ernest Thompson Seton

For several decades, readers throughout the world have enjoyed the books of Ernest Thompson Seton, Scottish-born naturalist, writer, painter and co-founder of the Boy Scouts of America. Although he was a prolific artist, his paintings, most of which are on exhibit at the Seton Museum in Cimarron, New Mexico, are not so widely known. In the hope of making Seton's art more available to the general public, Knopf decided to publish a collection of his sketches, oils and watercolors.

Knopf art director Bob Scudellari describes the project as a collaborative effort from the very beginning. As is the case with most art books, the editors offered advice about cropping, enlarging and emphasis, and Scudellari, who designed the book jacket, worked closely on all facets of the publication with the book's designer, Louise Fili, and production manager Ellen McNeilly. "Since I was involved with the initial conceptual development of the book," he explains, "it would have been strange to forego the design of the cover, which is the most important aspect of the total packaging." It was obvious that the jacket should make use of one of Seton's paintings, and Scudellari's first sketch incorporated an illustration of a hawk. The editors, however, felt that Seton was better known for his drawings of animals, so Scudellari proposed another design based on one of Seton's best-known works, a dramatic portrait of Lobo the wolf. Using the head of an

open-mouthed, fierce-looking beast on the cover of a book aimed at what is referred to in the trade as the "Bambi market" was something of a gamble, but the design was enthusiastically approved. Scudellari credits the popularity of *Jaws* and the ubiquitous shark image with creating the climate for the cover's acceptance. "Five years ago, it would have been considered too violent and bloody," he remarks. Joe Ramer, who did the mechanical and final lettering, extended Seton's beige background to accommodate the title. To get the best reproduction for the available money, the jacket was printed in Italy.

Above: back of book jacket; opposite page and below: illustrations by Seton used on jacket.

Publisher: Alfred A. Knopf, Inc.
Art director/designer: R. D. Scudellari
Illustrator: Ernest Thompson Seton
Letterer: Joe Ramer

Taoism is a Chinese religion and philosophy based on the concept that man must give up striving and through mystical contemplation attain an ideal state of being in which he will be free of desire and sensory experience, which are illusory. According to the Columbia Encyclopedia, "The Tao in the broadest sense is the way the universe functions, the path taken by natural elements. It is characterized by spontaneous creativity and by regular alternations of phenomena (day following night) that proceed without effort. Effortless action may be illustrated by the conduct of water, which unresistingly accepts the lowest level and yet wears away the hardest substance." These are the ideas which the book *Living Tao: Still Visions and Dancing Brushes* sets forth in the form of a photographic essay and single lines of poetry.

For the cover, art director Brenton Beck felt that there were two possibilities—either a strong graphic design based on typography or a photograph chosen from the material inside the book. Because of its reflected space, clarity, and sense of universal serenity (conditions which suggest the nature of Tao), he settled on the latter, a picture of the author/calligrapher Al Chung-liang Huang. Chung-liang, whose mystical observations—"sitting quietly doing nothing," "stillness in motion," "the inner mountain"—complement the photographs, painted the symbol which appears at the top, a character meaning the great void. "We reached a

verbal agreement on what our design approach would be long before physical work began on the project," Beck reports. "Because of this advance brainstorming, we were able to dispense with our usual preliminary design steps of roughs, layouts and comps and go directly to film. The first visual our client saw was the Color Key." Printed in full-color, the photograph glows with the brilliant blue of the sky. The symbol is dropped out in white.

Living TAO

Client: Celestial Arts
Design firm: Fifth Street Design Associates, Berkeley, CA
Art director: Brenton Beck
Designers: Al Chung-liang Huang, Brenton Beck
Photographer: Si Chi Ko
Letterer: Al Chung-liang Huang

Above: calligraphy from back of book jacket; below: spread from book.

I, Claudius/ Claudius the God

When Mobil Oil, which underwrites the Public Broadcasting System program Masterpiece Theater, commissioned Seymour Chwast to design a poster announcing the *I, Claudius* dramatizations, they asked that he base his illustration on British designer Richard Bailey's titles for the BBC/ London Film Productions television presentation. Chwast didn't mind not being able to start from scratch. "It's a good marketing idea and I wish I had thought of it to begin with," he confesses. Taking as his point of departure the somewhat obvious concept of the mosaic floor and the snake, Chwast added the goblet and the spilled, blood-colored wine to suggest the evil-doing of the story.

More or less simultaneously, Vintage Books, publisher of the original Robert Graves novels (*I, Claudius* and *Claudius the God*) on which the TV episodes were based, decided to reissue the two paperbacks with new covers using the same design. Mobil agreed and Chwast adapted his layout to include the author's name. On the cover of the second book, the mosaic pieces have rearranged themselves into the face of an older Claudius, and the broken Roman staff replaces the wine and the snake as a symbol of violence. Fifteen hundred copies of the poster were printed for display in Manhattan bus shelters and for use as promotion.

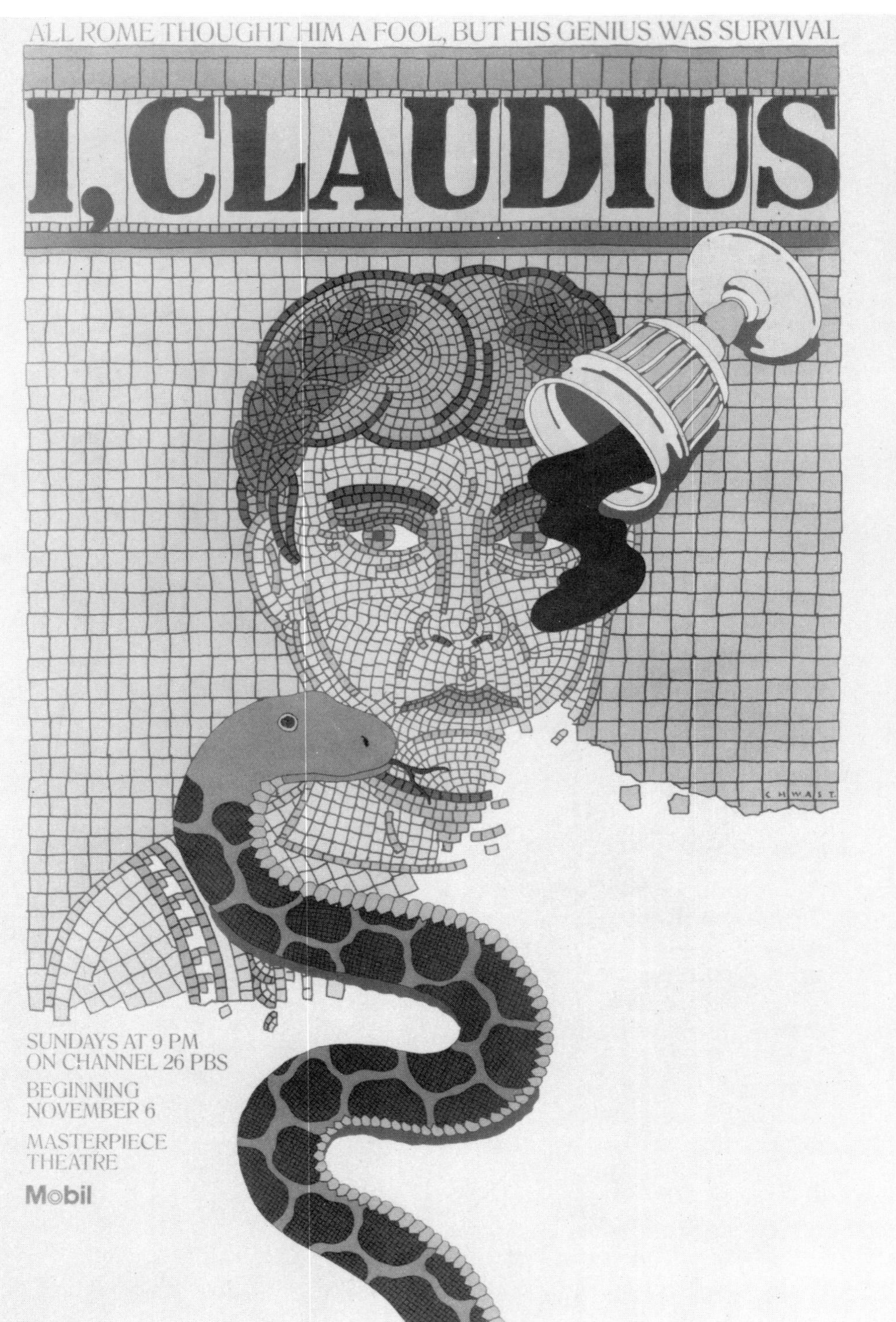

Client: Mobil Oil Co.
Art director: Gordon Bowman
Design firm: Push Pin Studios, New York
Designer/illustrator: Seymour Chwast
Printer: Crafton Printing Co.
Colors: Full color
Size: 24″ by 36″

394-72537-9
$3.95 / V-537
ROBERT GRAVES
CLAUDIUS THE GOD

Publisher: Vintage Books
Art director: Judith Loeser
Design firm: Push Pin Studios, New York
Designer/illustrator: Seymour Chwast

The Push Pin Graphic is a bimonthly magazine with an appreciative audience of art directors, designers, and other visually-oriented folk. Its editorial content is offbeat—the collective imaginative effort of editors and staff—and its pages serve as mobile exhibition space for a raft of talented Push Pin Studios artists.

Seymour Chwast's cover for an issue devoted to "Mothers" was put together with the special wit and inventiveness that are the province of a designer who knows that no one is looking over his shoulder and that his audience is an in-crowd. Rendered in colored pencil, cello-tac, and airbrush, the mother is pink and soft and huggable. But her eyes (inspired by an old German découpage of the devil) are green and her horns are sharp. "The art for the baby was a last-minute pick-up from an old postcard," Chwast remarks. "The striking resemblance to the mother was coincidental." This issue marks the beginning of a standardized format for Push Pin Graphic, whose previous covers were subject only to the inclinations of individual designers.

Publisher/design firm: Push Pin Studios, New York
Art director/designer/illustrator: Seymour Chwast

Opposite: illustrations from Push Pin Graphic. Clockwise from top left: Paul Gauguin's mother by David Croland; Juan Gris' mother by Seymour Chwast; Edvard Munch's mother by Fred Marshall; Aubrey Beardsley's mother by Milton Glaser.

Ma Mére

LA MADRI
OATS

M Θ M

FM
M O R

Unknown Man No. 89

Following the premise that a book jacket is a small poster which functions as a point-of-purchase sales tool, Lawrence Ratzkin designed a cover for *Unknown Man No. 89* which is dynamic, easily interpreted and unusual enough to make it stand out from the competition. Supplied with the manuscript and told not to use more than three colors, Ratzkin was given two weeks to come up with an appropriate graphic solution. Drawing his inspiration from the story, a straightforward mystery that gets underway with the discovery of an unidentified corpse, Ratzkin decided to illustrate the events rather than interpret them. Once he had zeroed in on the concept, he had only to assemble the necessary components: an ink print of his own bare foot and a reasonable facsimile of a morgue tag.

Publisher: Delacorte Press
Art director: Ann Spinelli
Designer: Lawrence Ratzkin

Detroit Public Radio 25th Birthday

In response to one of Detroit Radio's annual fund-raising appeals, Jennifer Clark, a devotee of the station's diverse and informative programming, offered to donate, instead of money, her time and design skills. A graduate student in design at the Cranbrook Academy of Art, Clark was involved in a work/study program which encouraged students to seek freelance clients among worthy local non-profit organizations. Collaborating with Stuart Hyke, development director of WDET, which accepted her offer enthusiastically, Clark set about designing a poster which would serve not only as an announcement of the station's 25th anniversary but also as an appeal to new listeners. Because the audience seemed from all reports to be fairly intellectual, Clark was able to indulge in a graphic solution which she describes as Swiss but eclectic. "It really came out of my school environment," she says; "I was very much influenced by my peers and my instructors." The copy is used not only to impart information but also as an illustrative element. Two balanced, flush-left Helvetica paragraphs at the top spread out into a melange of typefaces marching symmetrically forward on the page like a carefully spaced parade. "It's a play on early American advertising," Clark explains, "because it's centered and formal, but using modern elements." The split-font colors going from red and orange at the top to a dark green "birthday" add a touch of frivolity.

Client: WDET-FM, Detroit
Art director/designer: Jennifer Clark
Copywriter: Stuart Hyke
Printer: Lone Pine Press
Colors: Split font of green, yellow, red.
Size: 12″ by 23″

Albert

When Kevin Eggers of Utopia Records decided to produce a poster promoting blues-guitarist Albert King's newest release, he veered away from standard album publicity in favor of something more original. To make an effective noise amid the visual din of competitive posters, the King promotion, Eggers resolved, must be larger than life.

Assigning the task to Milton Glaser, who had often worked on Eggers' projects in the past, was both practical and inspired. Working from three or four good photographs of King taken by Norman Sieff, Glaser painted a relatively small portrait (12″ by 18″). Rendered in watercolor, colored pencil and some opaque pigment—an unusual combination of techniques for Glaser, who rarely mixes media—the illustration is one of intense contrasts. Light clothing frames the dark face; the clarity and candor of the mouth deepen the shadow obliterating the eyes. Seen at a distance, the image is three-dimensional, almost photographic; at close range, it becomes abstract shapes, pieces of color—according to Glaser, "a jumble of little scribbles." The drama of the close-up, dynamic enough in its original dimensions, is magnified with every square inch of its enlargement. It is an effect which appeals to Glaser. "I always like drawings to be enlarged," he remarks; "it gives them a totally different aspect. It intensifies the energy."

Client: Kevin Eggers/Utopia Records
Art director/designer: Milton Glaser
Printer: Gugler Lithographic
Colors: Full color
Size: 42″ by 63″

Space Diver

"The Plain Jane dress line is geared toward the junior customer, who's somewhere between 18 and mid-30s," says Helie Robertson, merchandise manager of Esprit de Corp., a California clothing manufacturer. "It's really more a state of mind than an actual age group," she continues, with a generous if pragmatic attitude certain to cheer female shoppers approaching their forties. To promote that Plain Jane image—a loose, unconventional, contemporary look that the logo by itself does not imply—Esprit de Corp. decided to produce a series of posters for display in sales showrooms and for retailers carrying Plain Jane dresses. Esprit de Corp. president Doug Tompkins approached photographer Richard Shaefer with the project. No time limit was imposed and Shaefer was given complete freedom to create a series of shots which would reflect the feeling of the clothing. "He didn't want catalog shots," Shaefer says, "he wanted a mood."

Using his own original photographic language, Shaefer put together out-of-the-ordinary but oddly coherent arrangements of everyday activities (diving, hanging up wash, repairing a truck, going to work), airborne vehicles (blimp, trapeze, flying dress) and, of course, a girl in Plain Jane attire presented informally, even negligently, as if the garment's distinguishing features were of no special account. Space Diver, the first poster in the series, is typical of Shaefer's method. The girl was shot lying down on the floor of Shaefer's studio. The diving board was taken, obviously, next to a swimming pool. Some of the clouds were part of a third photograph, but a good many of them were created by Shaefer himself, who slips easily into the role of illustrator when the mood strikes him. The final collage was hand-painted in oils, dyes and colored pencils, giving it a warm but delicately pastel finish. To reproduce the color exactly as it appeared in the original, the poster was printed in five colors with a tint varnish of 10 per cent yellow over all.

Client: Esprit de Corp.
Art director/designer: Richard Shaefer
Type designer: Doug Tompkins
Printer: Mike Roberts Color
Colors: Five colors with 10 per cent yellow tint varnish
Size: 24½" by 37½"

The character of Anna Karenina appealed to illustrator John Collier. Aloof, serious, brooding, her mood seemed to reflect some corner of his own personality. "I'm interested in portraying the melancholy in people," he observes, "the pensiveness and the joy and all the emotions they experience. I look at this individual I'm painting and I try to paint him so that when he looks back at me from the painting, there's something emotionally satisfying about it. In a sense, I put onto that person the emotional quality I want to feel myself." Doing a portrait of the Russian heroine for a poster promoting the Public Broadcasting System dramatization of the Tolstoy novel (on Masterpiece Theater) was, consequently, a welcome assignment.

Collier was supplied with 4 by 5 transparencies, 35mm slides and a black-and-white photograph of the actress playing Anna in costume. His final illustration, however, was a composite of various bits and pieces: the fur hat from one photograph, the dress from another which ended at the knees, the bottom of the skirt from Collier's imagination, and the sleeves from a still-life set-up. "There were some problems with the sleeves—the way the folds go when her arms are drawn up. It didn't look right in the photographs," Collier recalls, "so I reproduced it in the studio." The final portrait was done in pastels, a somewhat out-of-fashion medium which Collier enjoys and uses in a masterly fashion. Spraying the delicate surface turns the whites transparent, however, so the finish must be kept under glass and removed only for shooting. Designer Seymour Chwast, with Collier's concurrence, decided on the final size and position of the picture and added a headline with "K" and "A's" inspired by the letterforms of the Cyrillic alphabet.

Client: Mobil Oil Co.
Art director: Gordon Bowman
Design firm: Push Pin Studios, New York
Designer: Seymour Chwast
Illustrator: John Collier
Printer: Crafton Printing Co.
Colors: Full color
Size: 24″ by 36″

Endangered!

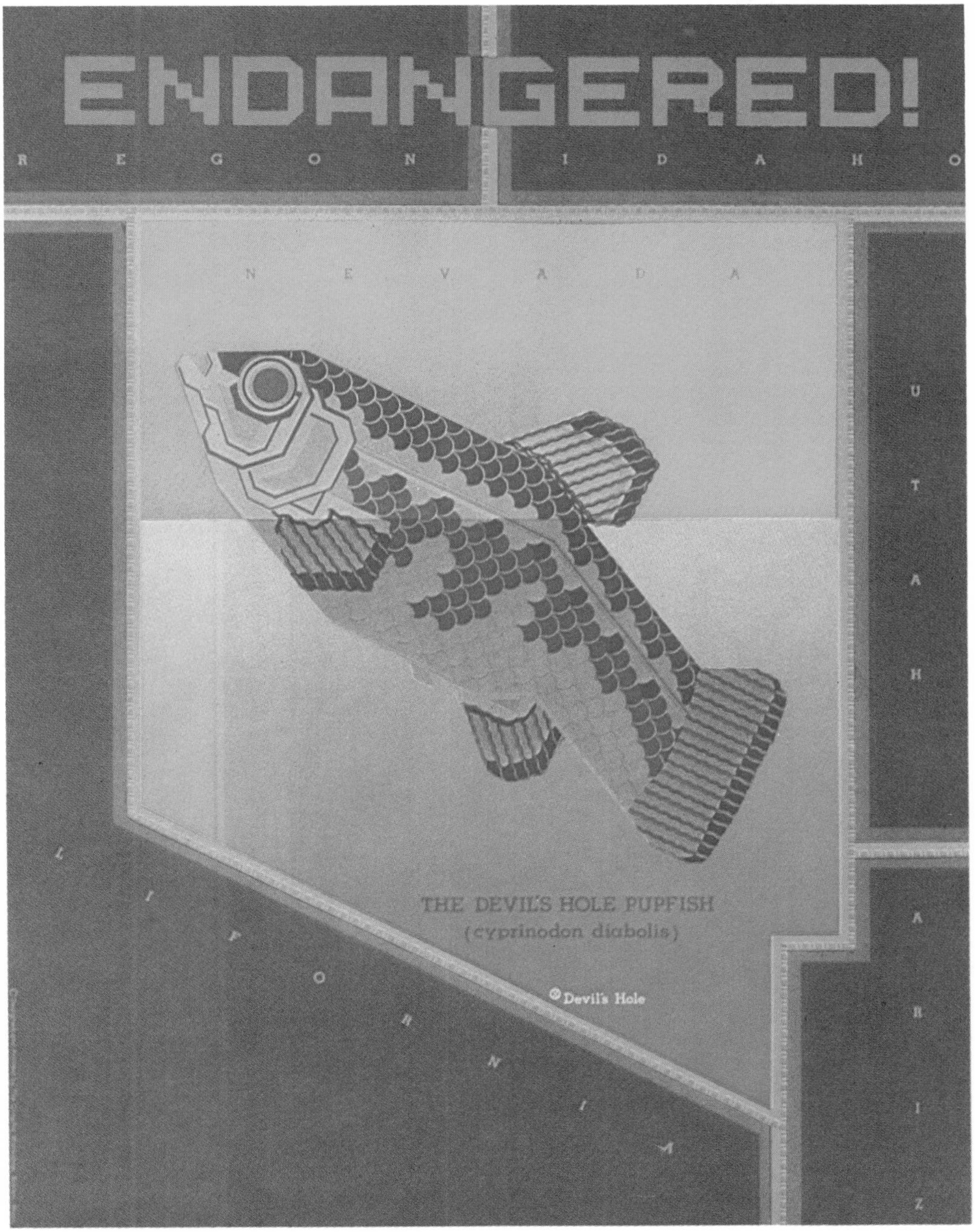

The Graphic Workshop is a silkscreen printing company owned and operated by five artists who function as printers, designers, illustrators, typesetters and copywriters. One of their current projects is the production of an annual series of endangered-species posters. Originally commissioned by the International Society for the Protection of Animals, the series has been continued by the Workshop members, who are concerned about conservation and feel that it makes an excellent peg on which to hang their interest in reviving the silkscreened poster as an art form.

Jack Weiner's carefully researched pupfish, the fifth production in the series, is rendered in luminous blues against the warm yellow, brown and rose of the American southwest. "During thousands of years of evolution," Weiner reports, "as the climate became dryer and dryer, the pupfish shrank from the size of a salmon to the size of a minnow. The last of the surviving species can be found today only in Devil's Hole, Nevada, a water-filled crevice fed by a spring. Legislation has recently been passed to prohibit drilling for water in that area, a process which affects the level of the water table, so that pupfish have a better chance to survive now than they have for many years."

Weiner's source material included a film provided by the India Ink Gallery, Santa Monica, California, an organization similarly concerned with fine art and the protection of the environment. He originally conceived the design to include a grid background, with the modular geometric pattern repeating the linear configuration of the contiguous states. "It was a graphic idea I had been working with for a long time," Weiner explains, "but it was too busy and basically an unnecessary element, so I abandoned it." The poster has been displayed in California and Massachusetts, and Workshop members intend to distribute it to a larger audience in hopes that it will inspire viewers to become more involved in conservation.

Client: India Ink Gallery
Design firm: The Graphic Workshop, Boston
Art director: Robert P. Moore
Designer: Jack Weiner
Printer: The Graphic Workshop
Colors: Serascreen—15 colors
Size: 20½" by 26½"

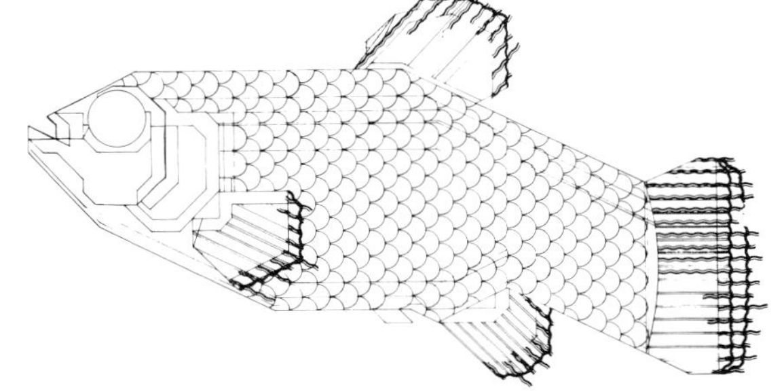

Left: sketch for fish; above: another poster in series.

Streamers/
For Colored Girls

The New York Shakespeare Festival, a non-profit organization guided with taste, imagination and vitality by producer Joseph Papp, was already an established city institution praised for its distinguished off- and on-Broadway productions when its agency, Case and McGrath, decided that a good reputation wasn't enough. To put forward an image as dramatic and noteworthy as the shows themselves, Gene Case and art director Reinhold Schwenk suggested that Papp commission a highly respected artist to do a poster for his next play. Papp's meeting with Paul Davis and the resulting poster for his production of *Hamlet* at the Vivian Beaumont Theater during the Festival's tenure at Lincoln Center are now past history. But the poster series, which revitalized the entire concept of theater advertising, has continued in a steady stream of inspired visual applause.

One of the most startling of Davis's designs is his painting for the David Rabe play *Streamers.* "'Streamers' is the term paratroopers use for parachutes that refuse to open," explains Davis, "and is a metaphor in this play for the failure of human relationships."

Avoiding a hackneyed army-barracks approach, Davis decided to suggest the violence of the play in a stop-action painting that depicts the terror of falling. Dressed in a pair of old army fatigues and sneakers (he couldn't find his boots), Davis lay on the floor of his living room and, without being able to see himself in order to judge the effect, assumed a variety of falling poses while his wife took Polaroid pictures. The painting he did from this source material became even more jarring when Schwenk suggested turning it upside down. "I liked it this way because the perspective was very strange," Davis remarks; "it's hard to get over your sense of gravity when you're painting." When Papp was told about the reversal, he quipped sympathetically, "That's just like taking the first act and putting it in the third."

Davis himself paints in the titles and most of the other lettering for his posters. For *Streamers,* he used a standard-size stencil for the headline and had a special stencil cut for the bottom three lines which were stripped in later.

Although he sometimes has little more to go on than a meeting with actors and director, Davis was able to see *For Colored Girls* at the Public Theater before it opened on Broadway. Abandoning his first sketch, a complicated design combining a rainbow with the title going all the way around the edge, he settled on the portrait of a black woman against a white wall covered with colorful graffiti. Schwenk suggested the subway tile and Papp insisted that the portrait, originally based on Davis's photo of a black model, be the author, Ntosake Shange. "I did a lot of tracings to get the words in the right place," Davis recalls. "All those little things that wind up looking like accidents have to be figured out—getting it to drip

just right, spattering it. You end up doing each carefully planned casual letter three or four times."

Davis's paintings are reproduced not only as large three-sheet posters to be displayed on subway platforms and in suburban railway stations, but also in a smaller size for sale to collectors and as 1½" by 3" black-and-white newspaper ads. New York Shakespeare Festival's associate producer, Bernard Gersten, has described the Festival's relationship with Davis in an interesting comparison. "He is our Toulouse-Lautrec and we are his Moulin Rouge," Gersten says. "But it's more than that; Paul has the classics of the world to illustrate; all Lautrec had were can-cans."

Although Papp's association with Lincoln Center has come to an end, the Davis/Festival relationship has continued with such projects as a poster for Papp's Broadway production of *The Water Engine,* posters for free Shakespeare-in-the-Park, posters for the Festival's cabaret theater, and a city wall in Manhattan's Cooper Square.

Client: New York Shakespeare Festival
Agency: Case & McGrath, New York
Art director: Reinhold Schwenk
Illustrator: Paul Davis
Printer: King Display (TDI)
Colors: Full color
Size: 42" by 84"

Canadian Opera 1977

Heather Cooper's striking poster advertising the 1977 season of the Canadian Opera Company—an illustration so rich in theatrical imagery and dramatic effect that it gives the appearance of having been created quite spontaneously with never a competing idea—oddly enough got off to a number of false starts. Cooper's original thought was to do a picture of Pan, the Greek god of forests, pastures, flocks and shepherds. Basing her illustration on the portrait of a friend whose resemblance to Pan had always fascinated her, she did a rough sketch which was rejected because it looked too much like an advertisement for just one of the season's presentations, *The Magic Flute*. The client insisted that the poster, which was to appear in galleries, retail outlets, public buildings and exhibit sites throughout Toronto, be all-encompassing. The image had to illustrate in a general way the full range of the company's 1977 productions.

Cooper's second foray was into the world of dance. "I decided that I should do some sort of exotic figure—like Nijinsky," she recalls. Posing a friend in a whole series of unusual dance positions, which she photographed and used as source material, Cooper produced a new pencil sketch. "The problem this time was that it looked too much like dance and not enough like singing," she explains. "Even though I had drawn the figure with her mouth open and singing, it still wasn't enough."

The third try, inspired by tragic/comic theatrical masks which Cooper had always found appealing, was a success. Part fantasy, part fact, a conglomeration of ordinary everyday objects and the illustrator's vivid imagination, the project in many ways typifies Cooper's way of working. "Those seashells are my ashtrays," she explains; "the amber beads are my assistant's. They're all bits and pieces from around the office. I did use a face to bind in everything—I decorated somebody up so that I could get the folds and things right—but that face was nothing like what you see now. This is totally stylized... it wasn't to look like a person, it was to look like a mask." The head—at first glance it does not appear to be disembodied—floats against a background of tendrils and undergrowth, which, though drawn from Cooper's imagination, have their roots in the tangled damp of her own back garden.

"The poster continues to be distributed through fine arts distributors and poster shops," comments Cooper's partner, Robert Burns, "but the ultimate compliment is that more opera posters have been stolen in Toronto than ever before."

Client: Canadian Opera Co.
Design firm: Burns, Cooper, Hynes Ltd., Toronto
Art director/illustrator: Heather Cooper
Type designers: Heather Cooper, Robert Burns, Lawrence Finn
Printer: Herzig Somerville
Colors: Three process colors and two special reds
Size: 20″ by 29¾″

Raychem

When the Raychem Corporation reorganized its centrally combined operations into four separate divisions, it wasn't an entirely easy transition for the staff. To help smooth over the rough spots for disgruntled employees, especially for the salesmen who were dismayed to find that their clients seemed to have been reorganized along with the company, management embarked on a kind of public-relations-begins-at-home program. The Communications and Design Department was asked to produce a series of posters which would identify the four new divisions for the staff and serve also as wall decorations in Raychem offices all over the world. "We get 50 or 60 requests for wall decorations from sales offices every year," explains art director John Rieben; "they aren't allowed to go out and buy their own; their requests have to go through us." Posters featuring a handsome graphic image symbolizing the function of each of the new divisions—electronics, energy, process and telecommunications—seemed an ideal solution.

The geometric shape which appears on all the posters and provides a controlling motif for the series is a circle symbolizing the world. The designs within the circles are abstractions of physical shapes and processes. The electronics industry poster, preferred by Casebook jurors to the other three, features a regular pattern of triangles going from left to right and suggesting the movement of energy through the medium of electronic impulses. The poster was silkscreened in eight colors and Rieben notes that the overlays had to be very precisely cut to ensure perfect registry on each of the eight passes. Although the triangular pattern never varies, the random application of color creates a feeling of constant nervous movement and changing rhythms.

Rieben reports that reaction to the posters has been very favorable, with the result that the designs have been adapted for use as Raychem Quarterly Report covers. But what of the salesmen? It would be interesting to know if the project has really helped to soothe their unsettled corporate souls.

Client: Raychem Corp.
Art director/designer: John Rieben
Printer: Trend Graphics
Colors: Tan, two browns, two grays, two oranges, white
Size: 30″ by 42″

Anna Christie

Eugene O'Neill's play *Anna Christie* takes place on the waterfront in dim and shabby surroundings. The heroine is young, troubled, ostensibly out of place in the rough-and-tumble setting. The character and atmosphere invite pictorial recreation.

James McMullan's poster advertising the 1977 Broadway production of the play responds to that invitation most appealingly. Challenged by a lack of direction that allowed him the freedom to paint whatever he chose as long as his poster included a portrait of the actress Liv Ullmann, McMullan set about gathering the information he needed. Unable to attend a rehearsal, he read the play and discussed the project with costume designer Jane Greenwood, whose work he admired. "Unfortunately, by the time I talked to her I already had an idea of what I wanted to do," McMullan recalls, "and we disagreed about the color of Liv Ullmann's dress. She wanted it black and it wouldn't have worked in the illustration I had planned." In spite of Greenwood's objections, McMullan went ahead with his original idea. Asking a friend to pose for him in an old bar in Little Italy in downtown Manhattan, he set up a convincing scene that would serve as the model for the basic elements in his painting. Research photos of Liv Ullmann and his own imagination filled in the details. Technical happenstance, however, provided the solution to one of McMullan's stickiest problems—the combination of

Left and opposite page, above: preliminary sketches; opposite page, below: research photos of model and actress Liv Ullmann.

the barroom setting with the watery expanse behind it. In his rough sketch, he indicated the dark area with a pencil scribble. "The gesture of that scribble had a certain energy that I liked," McMullan recalls. "I tried that kind of calligraphy with a brush and I found that it looked nice with a brush, too." In the past, McMullan had always combined two different realities with a merging factor like fog or mist. "But," he says, "I wanted to do one that was very bald—without the intervention of that sort of magic. I liked the straightforwardness of this."

Designed with the idea that the image should be simple but interesting enough to reward close and repeated viewing, the final painting is equally effective as a three-sheet poster, a window card, and a black-and-white newspaper ad.

Client: Alexander H. Cohen
Design firm: Visible Studio, New York
Agency: Ash/LeDonne, Inc.
Art director: Jeff Ash
Designer/illustrator: James McMullan
Printer: Artcraft Lithograph & Printing Co.
Colors: Full color
Size: Three-sheet poster; 14" by 22⅛" window card

Saratoga/Declaration of Independence

Saratoga is one of the most recent in a handsome series of posters produced by the National Park Service in recognition of the U.S. Bicentennial celebration. The project, begun in 1976 and expected to continue for several years, entails the publication of booklets and posters commemorating the history of every major Revolutionary War battle site in America. Illustrator Alan Cober, who had finished the drawings for the Saratoga handbook by the time the poster was commissioned, was already inundated with source material, including scholarly commentaries, historical portraits, costume drawings and reference supplied by the Park Service. To conjure up a more vivid impression of the 1777 battle which marked the turning point of the Revolution, he decided to visit Saratoga and make sketches of the battlefield. The resulting illustration rendered in pen and colored inks is a detailed, episodic panorama designed to be studied at close range. "Because the poster was intended as a keepsake, we could indulge in a long text," observes Nick Kirilloff, chief of graphics for the Park Service publication division. The written captions describing important incidents and principle participants were the artist's idea. Surfacing here and there in nervous patches, this kind of graphic commentary has become a hallmark of Cober's work, as personal and readily identifiable as his signature.

Other not-so-recognizable signatures provide the motif for a second Park Service poster designed with customary brilliance and wit by Saul Steinberg. "We wanted a Steinberg poster in the series," relates art director Vincent Gleason, "and Ivan Chermayeff, because of his large collection of Steinberg art and his long association with the artist, pursued it for us." Asked simply to do a poster

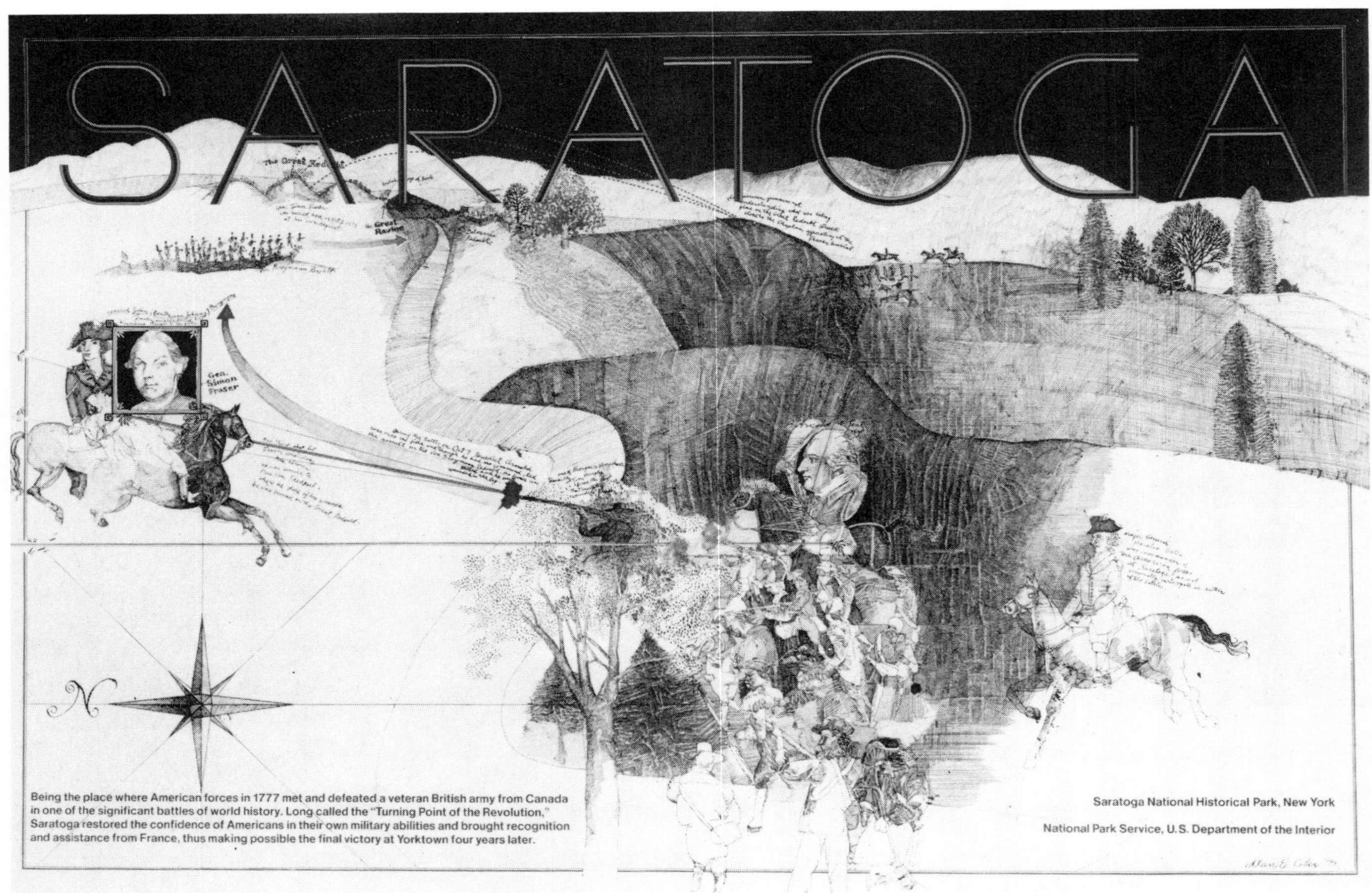

Client: National Park Service, U.S. Department of the Interior
Art director: Vincent Gleason
Designers: Nicholas Kirilloff, Dennis McLaughlin
Illustrator: Alan E. Cober
Copywriters: Heath Pemberton, Ray Baker
Printer: Government Printing Office
Colors: Full color
Size: 42″ by 28″

about the Declaration of Independence, Steinberg created yellowed documents, official looking seals, and illegible calligraphic swashes laden with the personalities of their unseen writers to suggest that every individual must sign his own subjective declaration of independence. Chermayeff reports that, having drawn the intentionally ambiguous scrawl at the top (an eagle? a dove? some hint of Thomas Jefferson?) with his own little wooden pen, the artist then signed that very pen and made it part of his composition.

The final production of the poster was as unusual as its concept. All the various components were delivered separately and had to be stripped together on film by the processing house in Milwaukee.

Printed in preliminary editions of 5000 and reprinted as often as the demand warrants, Park Service posters serve both as promotion for the historic landmarks they depict and as souvenirs for sightseers. In a gratifying tribute to the good taste and intelligence of the general public, and in spite of predictions to the contrary (Gleason reports that the bureaucracy hated the design), the Steinberg poster has produced record sales. Originally offered in museum shops in Philadelphia, along with a Leonard Baskin poster of Benjamin Franklin and a Chermayeff poster of the Liberty Bell, the Steinberg sold more than twice as well as the others, an unprecedented 350 copies in the first month.

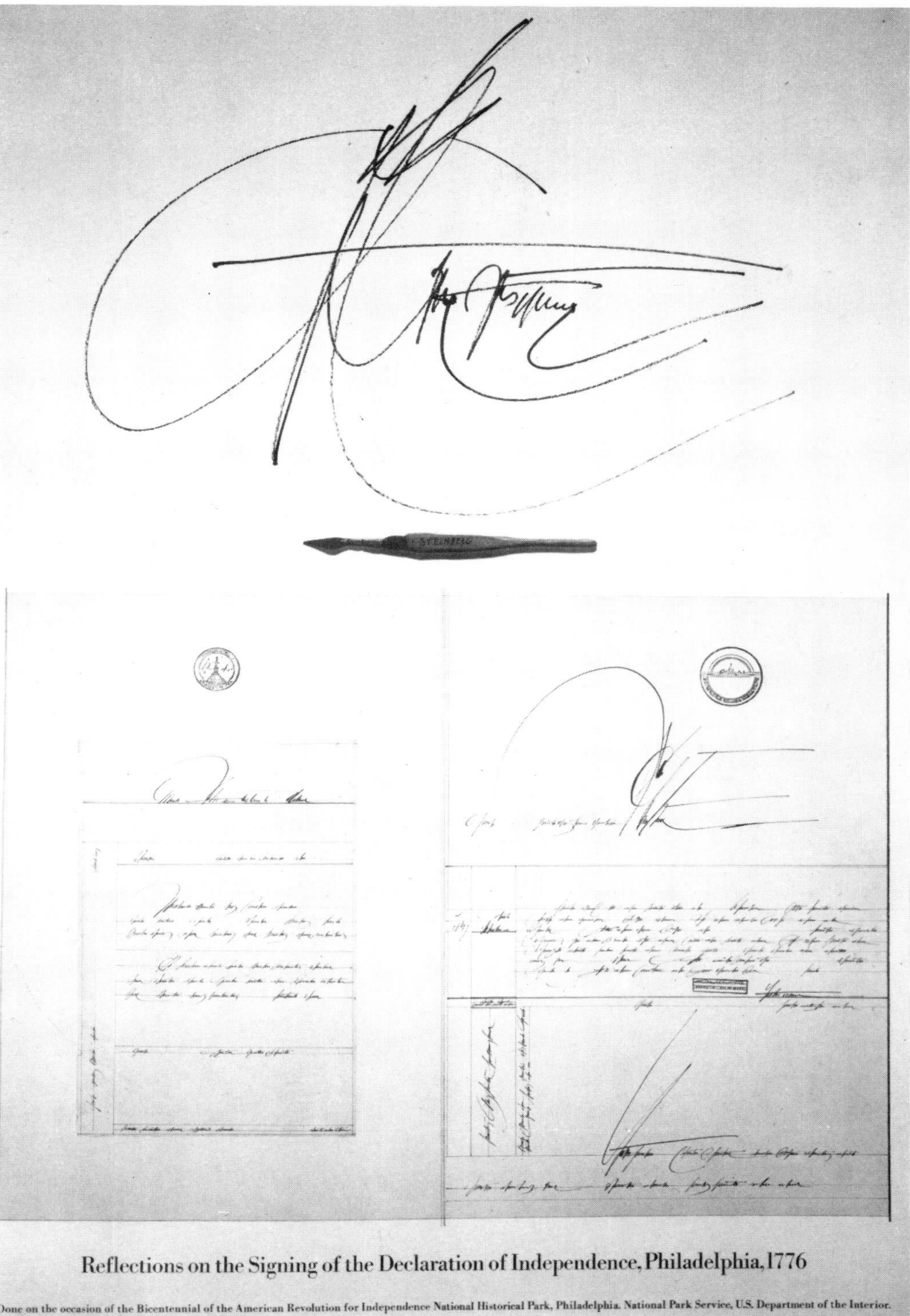

Client: National Park Service, U.S. Department of the Interior
Art director: Vincent Gleason
Design firm: Chermayeff & Geismar, New York
Illustrator: Saul Steinberg
Printer: Government Printing Office
Colors: Full color
Size: 28″ by 42″

School of Visual Arts

Film School

Every year the School of Visual Arts publications department puts out a number of promotion pieces to attract new students. Mailed to guidance counselors in secondary schools and junior colleges all over the country for posting on bulletin boards, they serve not only as advertisements of SVA programs and opportunities but also as examples of exceptional student work. To promote the film school, the publications department, working with Media Arts co-chairman Richard Wilde, decided to produce a poster headlined "Art is more than a brush on canvas." "When high school students think of art, they think of a brush and canvas, not all the other areas it encompasses," explains Wilde. "We wanted to educate them to realize that film is considered an art form. Editing, script-writing, directing, photography—all of it is really art within a different medium." Wilde, acting as art director for the project, called on five or six top senior students and asked them to come up with an illustration to fit the copy. Beat Keller's inspired colored-pencil rendering of a palette which becomes a film strip worked best. The image describes a double metamorphosis. Reading down, the pots of color turn into film. Reading across, each series of pictures illustrates action. The sun sets; the sun rises; a bird flies. Susan Cullen Eckrote, a former student now employed as a designer on the publications department staff, supplied the camera logo at

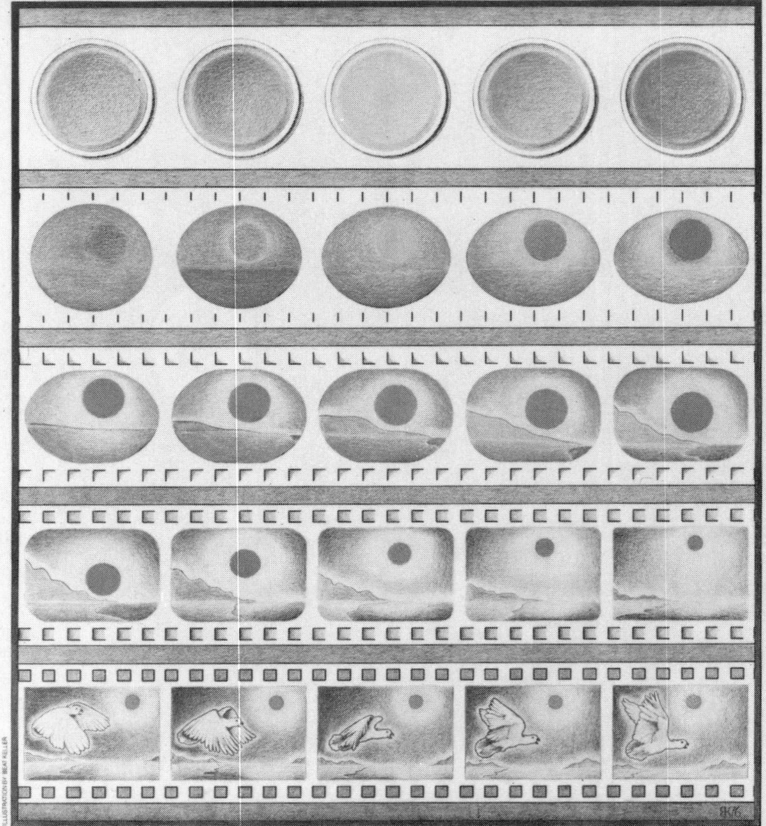

Client: School of Visual Arts Publications Department
Art director: Richard Wilde
Designer: Susan Cullen Eckrote
Illustrator: Beat Keller
Copywriter: Dee Ito
Printer: Visual Arts Press
Colors: Full color
Size: 16¾" by 22"

the bottom. "It was quite a job," Wilde recalls, "to reduce a super-complex piece of machinery to a two-dimensional black-and-white motif."

A second publications department poster illustrates SVA's familiar headline, "Having a talent isn't worth much unless you know what to do with it." When this copy is used on subway posters, school policy requires that they be designed by a member of the teaching staff. However, for a school poster announcing an examination for scholarship candidates, Wilde wanted a student illustrator. Since the competition is rigorous—1000 students apply for 12 awards in a two-and-a-half-hour exam and portfolio review—Wilde felt it was important for the copy to be illustrated with an upbeat, positive image. Ron DiSenza's high-wire artist offers just the right combination of skill and insouciance.

Wilde reports that the poster was successful on several counts. Not only did it elicit favorable response from the SVA staff and from high schools where it was displayed; it also provided DiSenza with professional experience and an excellent printed portfolio piece.

Client: School of Visual Arts Publications Department
Art directors: Silas Rhodes, Richard Wilde
Designer: Susan Cullen Eckrote
Illustrator: Ron DiSenza
Printer: Visual Arts Press
Colors: Full color
Size: 14¼″ by 22½″

Sports: The 21st Century

An important part of any design student's education is a certain amount of practical experience working with professional clients. In recent years, the School of Visual Arts in Manhattan has been able to offer students this kind of experience through the auspices of a prominent typesetter and photoengraver, the Master Eagle Family of Companies, which holds an annual exhibit of Media Arts students' work. The arrangement is mutually beneficial. It gives the students an opportunity to show their work and have those pieces which are selected as announcements and invitations professionally printed. It gives the school's educational programs favorable publicity. And it gives Master Eagle the chance to attract clients with a lively show of graphics and handsomely designed mailers which serve as samples of the company's services.

The idea behind the 1977 show, "Sports: the 21st Century," was inspired. Hundreds of letters were sent off to prominent athletes asking them to predict the future of sports. When the answers came back, senior students were asked to illustrate what these well-known personalities had described. "It was really a competition to see what paid off the line best," says Richard Wilde, who, with Media Arts co-chairman Marshall Arisman, was in charge of the project; "but the visual had to be able to stand by itself, too." Wilde reports that the students' solutions were so overwhelmingly successful that the choice of winner finally rested on which illustration would work best as a large poster. Although Marc Phelan's jockey riding a futuristic horse—in luminous green, orange and purple against a dark background—may not be everyone's vision of basketball star Earl Monroe's "space-age gladiator," it makes a powerful image on its own terms.

School of Visual Arts Presents:

SPORTS: THE 21ST CENTURY

We asked: "What changes do you see happening in sports by the 21st Century?" Illustrations, graphics and dimensional works by students based on predictions from fact to fantasy by famous sports personalities, sports fans and other students. An exhibition at the Master Eagle Gallery, 40 W. 25th St., 6th floor, April 15-May 13, 1977, from 10AM-12PM and 2PM-4PM, Monday through Friday.

Arthur Ashe	Ken Henderson	Earl Monroe	O.J. Simpson
Nick Buoniconti	Gordon Johncock	Mike Mosley	Stan Smith
Dick Butkus	Tom Landry	Merlin Olsen	Tom Sneva
Rod Gilbert	Lee Leonard	Nolan Ryan	Bart Starr
Janet Guthrie	Frank Mingo	Dick Schaap	Tom Weiskopf

"The 21st Century will be the age of the super-human athlete, the space-age gladiator...emphasis will be placed on breeding the best...'Rollerball' will become a reality."

School of Visual Arts

The School of Visual Arts in cooperation with The Master Eagle Family of Companies.

Client: School of Visual Arts; Master Eagle Family of Companies
Designer: Martha Savitzky
Art director: Richard Wilde
Illustrator: Marc Phelan
Copywriter: Dee Ito
Printer: Master Eagle
Colors: Full color
Size: 22¾" by 27¼"

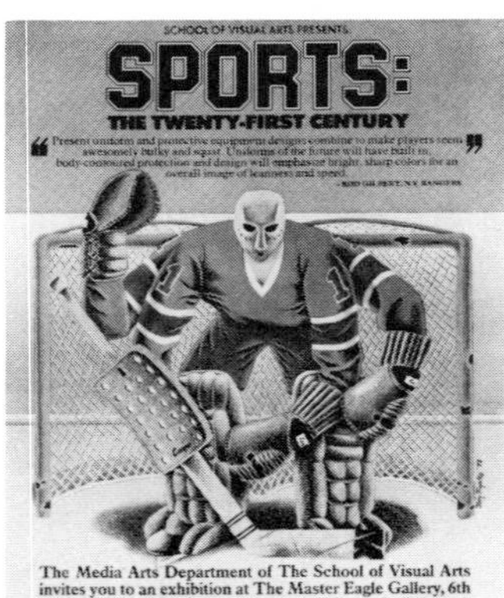

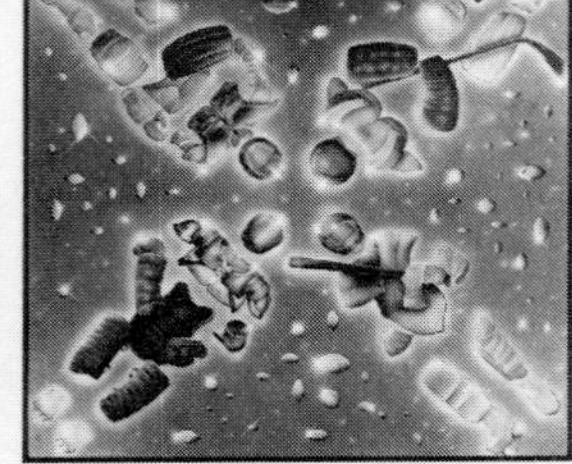

Right: student-illustrated invitations to exhibition and exhibition opening.

America Goes Metric

More down to earth in concept and general effect is another student poster, "America Goes Metric." In a second student/industry collaboration, Master Eagle decided to print a poster for use as a promotion piece and asked SVA to select a student designer. The company's choice of thematic material was purely informational, useful certainly, but a bit on the dry side. Imagination and superb technique were required to present it in an appealing manner. Chuck Albano, a fourth-year illustration student, and Penny Coleman, a graphics major, produced the final design as a combined term project. Albano, who was excused from illustration class to give him time for the additional work, based his drawings on information endorsed by the National Bureau of Standards. His tightly cross-hatched drawings, rendered with the finest rapidograph available and subsequently tinted with colored inks, turned what might have been a humdrum collection of scales and measuring tools into a fascinating exhibit of detailed instruments with the look of old engravings.

The project, on which Albano expended 240 hours of illustration time, has met with unprecedented success. Master Eagle has been flooded with requests for the poster in numbers varying from one to 250,000. Although most of the requests come from schools and universities, there have been letters from elderly ladies asking for a poster to send to their grandchildren, galleries who want the print in their collections, and companies who wish to buy reprint rights and produce the design in enormous quantities. Master Eagle as a matter of company policy refuses to sell the poster but will give it away as a public service in amounts up to 150 copies if they feel the cause is worthy. So far, they have issued 40,000 copies in four printings.

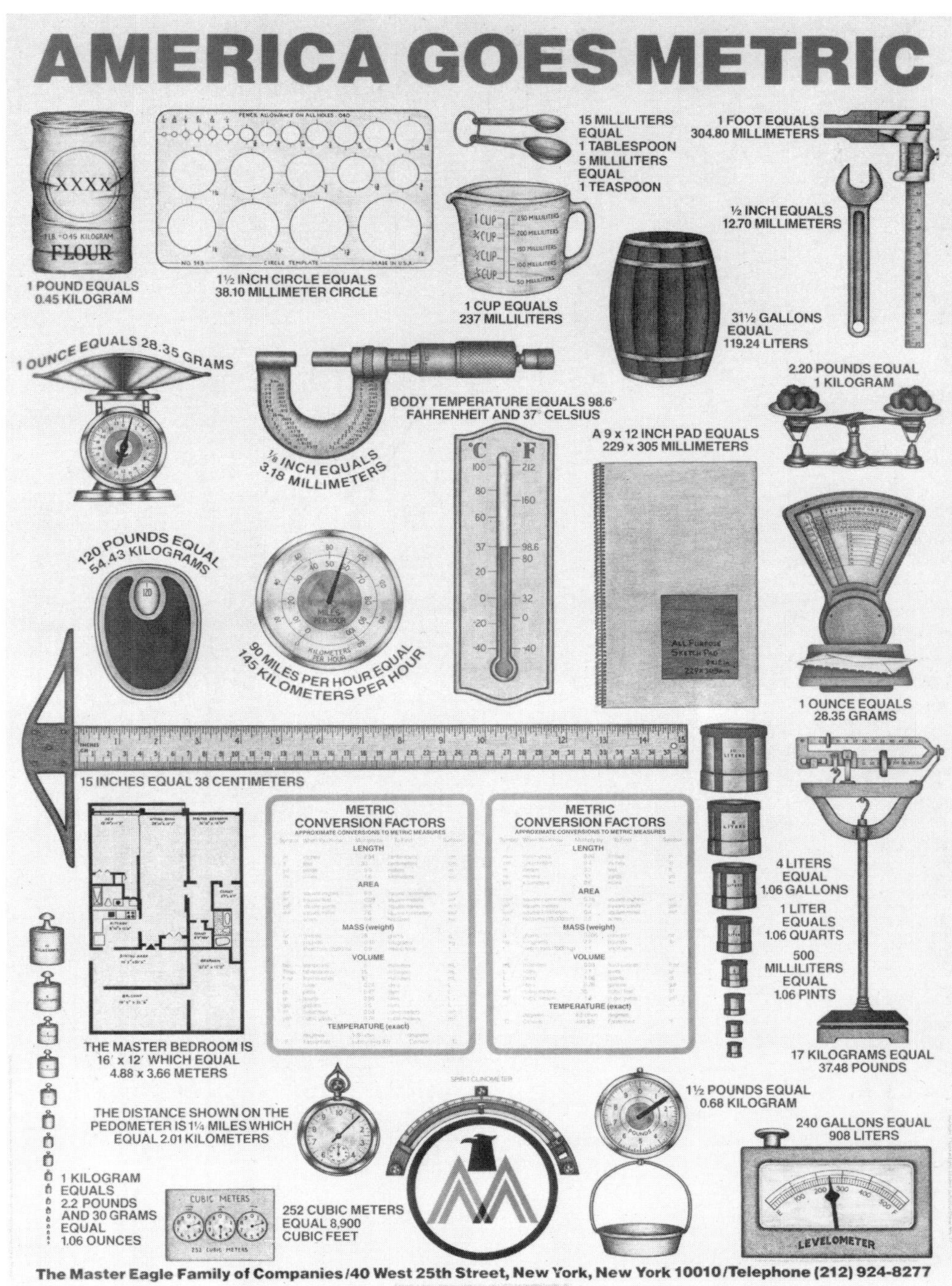

Client: Master Eagle Family of Companies
Art director/designer/ copywriter: Penny Coleman
Illustrator: Chuck Albano
Printer: Master Eagle
Colors: Full color
Size: 25″ by 34″

Corbin/Yamafuji & Partners

When the architectural firm Corbin/Yamafuji & Partners settled into new offices, they took advantage of the move to send out a poster which would serve not only as an address change notice but also as a promotion piece distinguished and subtle enough to avoid raising the eyebrows of the AIA. "Architects who are members of the AIA are not allowed to advertise," explains designer Jann Church, "so we decided to make a relocation announcement that would also get the philosophy of the firm across." Church had an anthology of statements by well-known architects and asked Corbin/Yamafuji to choose quotes which they thought were representative of their own outlook and standards. The three excerpts from the writings of Le Corbusier, Frank Lloyd Wright and Richard Neutra make a familiar frame of reference for clients, vendors, and consultants to whom the poster is mailed, and furnished Church with appropriate graphic elements on which to base her design. Wright, advocating simplicity and repose, warns against an excessive love of detail; Neutra urges taking advantage of the assets inherent in any natural site; and Le Corbusier's familiar dictum "form follows function" begins with the sentence, "Architecture is the masterly, correct and magnificent play of the masses brought together in light." Church's three-dimensional geometric forms and their light and shaded surfaces are virtual pictograms of Le Corbusier's quote. Printed in rust and yellow against a soft gray background, they accent the white blocks of copy in an abstract pattern that suggests the spatial and formal elements with which architects are concerned.

Client: Corbin/Yamafuji & Partners
Art director: Jann Church
Designers: Jann Church, Lisa Briner
Printer: Graphic Press
Colors: Five matching inks, plus gloss and dull varnish
Size: 13¼" by 38"

Grope Fest

Grope Fest, a phrase which seems to have strayed into the world of design from a local teen-age hangout and suggests a dimly-lit and sensuous orgy, is in reality nothing more than the name of a party given by The Architects Collaborative in May 1977 to commemorate Walter Gropius' birthday. The poster announcing this festive occasion, and inviting TAC employees to attend, features a delicately balanced, Bauhaus-inspired organization of basic linear elements—an unfinished triangle, the circular motif of Gropius' architectural registration stamp, and the architect's photograph in a square frame. "Gropius was the founder of the Bauhaus years before founding our firm," explains Katherine Selfridge of TAC: "this was the obvious solution."

Designed and printed within two days for a budget of $100 (circumstances which influenced the decision to use existing photographic elements and simple shapes), the unusually large poster appeared not only in lobbies of the TAC building in Cambridge but also on the inside of double-opening elevator doors so that both halves came together as the doors closed. It was printed in an edition of six copies by the Swiss line dry-print method.

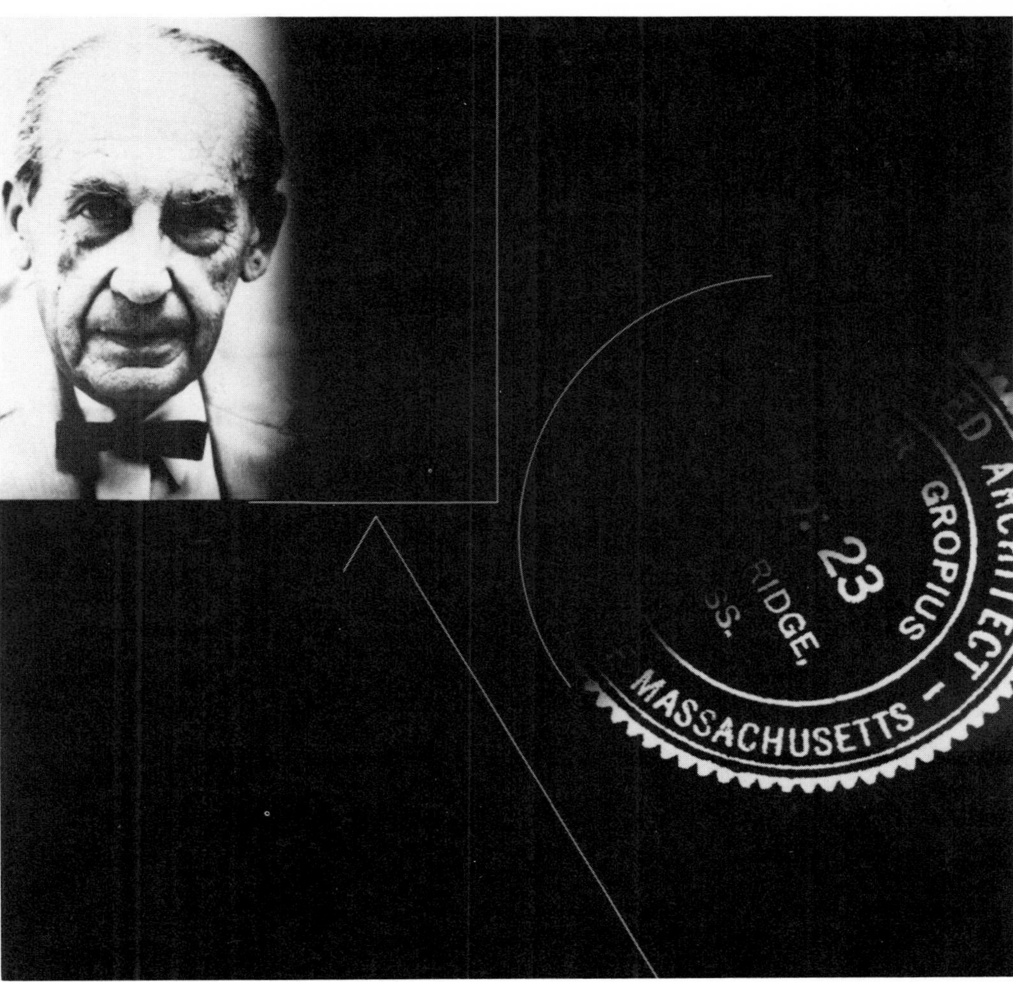

Client: The Architects Collaborative
Art director/designer: Harish Patel, TAC
Printer: Stone Reprographics
Colors: Black-and-white
Size: 32″ by 32″

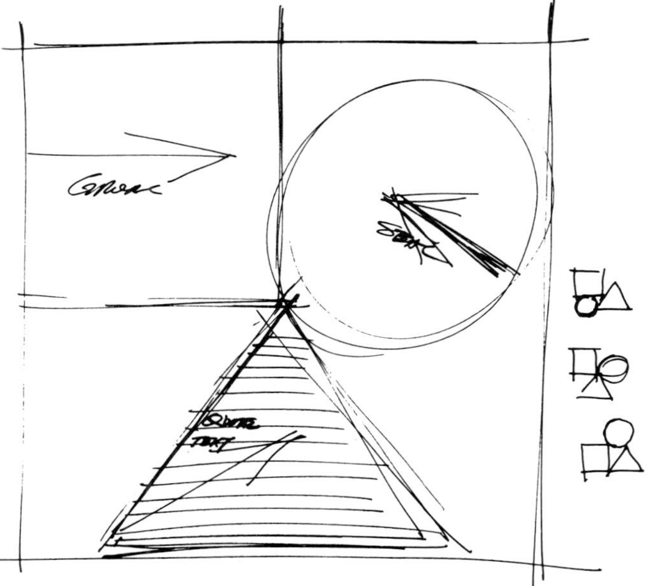

Right: preliminary sketch.

Fishes of the U.S.A.

Champion Papers' stunning series of promotion pieces called "Imagination" are rapidly becoming collectors' items. Handled from concept to finished product with grace and good judgment, each issue is as valuable for its richly illustrated and informative text as for its varied sampling of Champion papers and their capabilities.

"Imagination XX, Rivers U.S.A." is every bit as handsome as its predecessors. Produced in "celebration of several of the great American rivers," it included as an integral part of the package a poster illustrating the most common fishes found in American rivers and streams. Miho, who was responsible for the design of the entire booklet, originally wanted the poster to display some of the more unusual species. He thought they would make a particularly interesting and colorful exhibit. However, former Assistant Secretary of the Interior for Fish and Wildlife Nathaniel P. Reed, who was asked to make the final selection, reasoned that a montage of the most common fishes would be more useful to serious fishermen and general public alike. Miho asked San Francisco artist John Wyatt, whose detailed technique and skill with watercolors he admired, to do the painting. To satisfy his preference for working from life, Wyatt went to his local fish market, bought a sample of every variety, drew it, and then painted the entire collection to actual scale following Miho's rough layout. Miho reports that, although same-size art made routine handling a bit awkward, everyone was pleased with the result. The poster worked well both as a printing/papers demonstration and as a follow-up promotion piece for "Imagination XX."

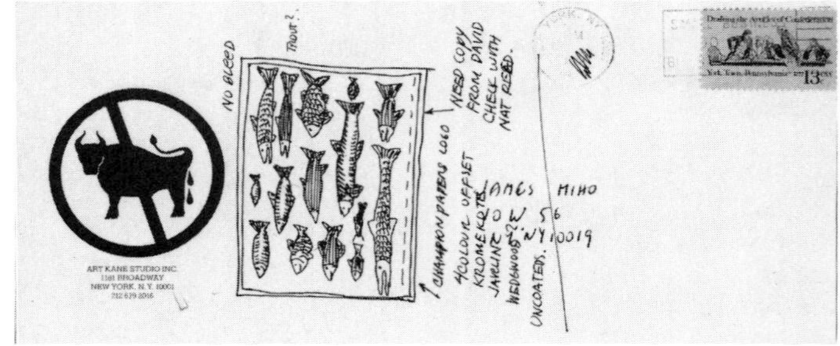

Above: Miho's sketch on envelope for illustrator John Wyatt.

Client: Champion Papers
Design firm: Miho, Inc., New York
Art director/designer: Miho
Illustrator: John Wyatt
Copywriter: David R. Brown
Printer: Rogers Offset
Colors: Full color
Size: 38″ by 28″

Work

The true measure of a designer's talent can be taken from the work he produces with limited resources. By this standard, Marc Treib, who rarely strays beyond a $25 limit, has established his expertise beyond the shadow of a doubt. The latest in his series of handsome low-budget designs is a poster announcing a lecture by Paul Friedberg to the students, faculty and staff of the Department of Architecture at the University of California at Berkeley. Friedberg is a New York landscape architect who specializes in parks and urban recreation areas. Treib's image is simple but striking—an urban skyline and a flower. The vertical placement of the logo at the bottom completes the flower's stem. To get texture from the diazo printing process, Treib used tracing paper on the original film positive in the area of sky behind the flower where he wanted a mottled tone to appear. Displayed on bulletin boards in the College of Environmental Design, the posters don't have to be viewed from a great distance. "Someone commented that the type was indistinct," Treib remarks, "but all its readers are pedestrians—they can move up to read it."

Client: Department of Architecture, University of California, Berkeley
Art director/designer: Marc Treib
Printer: Berkeley Blueprint
Colors: Brown-line or black-line diazo
Size: 18″ by 24″

Wayne Guthrie

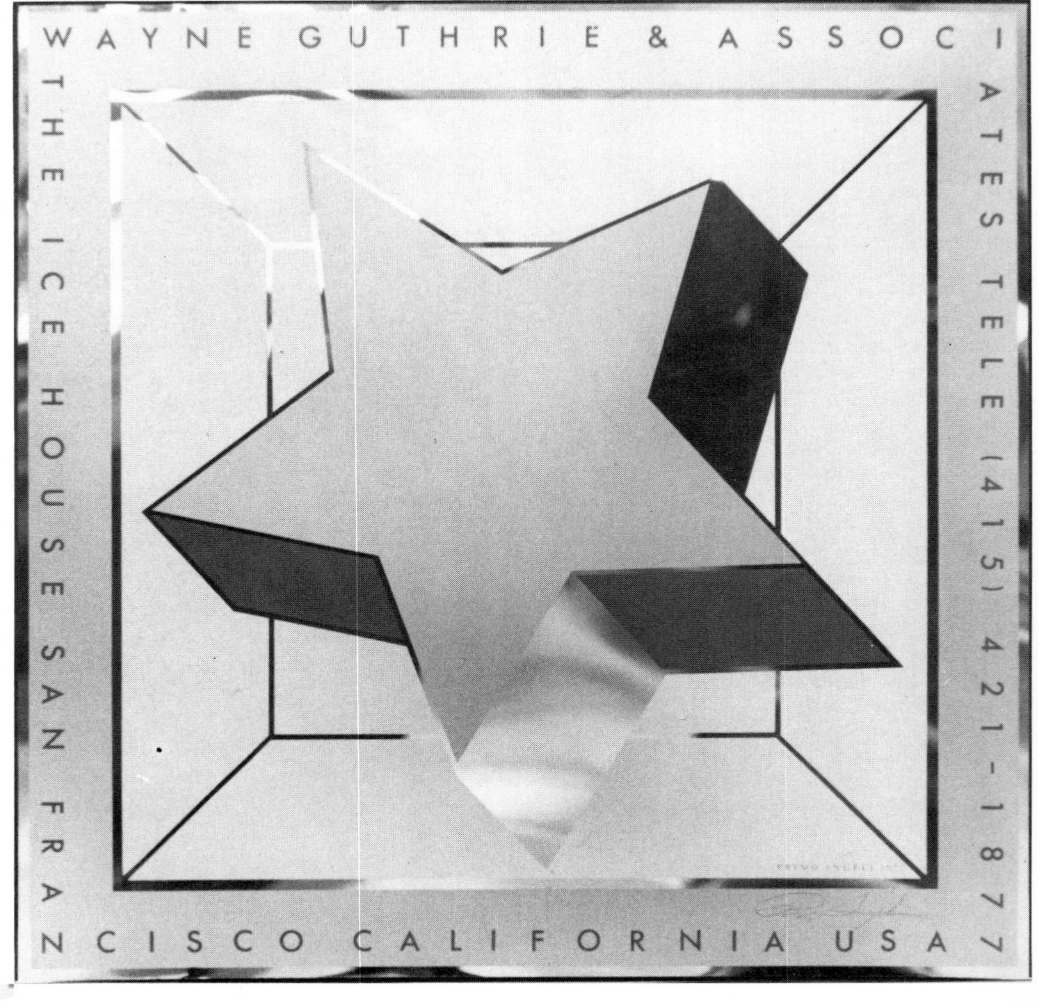

San Francisco's huge antique Ice House, saved from demolition and restored for contemporary use as a warehouse/showroom for architectural contract furnishings, has become one of the classiest addresses in the city. When Wayne Guthrie, a furniture dealer with Ice House offices, asked Primo Angeli to design a poster for him, Angeli felt it was important for the image to reflect that sophisticated setting. Although the poster was to function as an understated, soft-sell promotion piece, Angeli was concerned that it survive on its own as a striking and durable piece of art.

Since the poster was to be given to architects, buyers, designers of space, and top-name manufacturers of contemporary furniture, Angeli combined elements that would be familiar to a design-conscious audience. A three-dimensional star (suggesting "star" manufacturers) glitters in an open box-like square implying space. To intrigue viewers interested in color, material, and texture, Angeli printed the poster in two silver hues and one gray on silver mylar. The final image literally mirrors its environment by taking on the protective coloring of reflected surroundings.

Client: Wayne Guthrie and Associates
Art director/designer: Primo Angeli
Illustrator: John Gaccione
Typography: Rene Yung
Printer: The Works
Colors: Two silvers, one gray on silver mylar
Size: 24" by 24"

Black Nude

To announce a one-man show of his work at the Musées Royaux des Beaux-Arts in Brussels late in 1976, Milton Glaser produced a variation on one of his own themes, played for the first time about eight years previously, and to resounding applause. His poster for the "Big Nudes" exhibition at Visual Arts Gallery in 1968 is surely one of the most provocative designs in recent graphic history. What better inspiration for a new image which would serve not only to publicize the exhibit but also to identify the artist? "I have always wanted to use the nude in an iconographic way," Glaser explains. "I decided to up-date that poster ten years later, to see if I could do one that would be as effective, yet different."

Challenged both by the museum's low budget for the project and by his own decision to work in a horizontal format, Glaser has devised an image whose generous impact belies its economy of line and color. Printed in only two colors on inexpensive paper, the warm charcoal sensuality of "Black Nude" with its subtle whispers of brighter tone is the result of red overprinting green.

Client: Musées Royaux des Beaux-Arts de Belgique, Arte Moderne
Art director/designer: Milton Glaser
Printer: Metropolitan Printing
Colors: Red and green
Size: 36" by 24"

Right: Glaser's 1968 poster for "Big Nudes" exhibition.

For his elegant announcement of a Santa Cruz City Museum exhibition celebrating marine mammals—which include some of the most graceful and primitive aquatic creatures—designer Bill Prochnow resorted to graceful, old-fashioned techniques. "This poster was planned from the beginning as a limited edition broadside to be hand-printed on a Van der Cook proof press," he reports. "The press size limited the image area to less than full-sheet coverage; the type was hand-set; and the final illustration, which had to be reproduced by a relief printing process, was printed directly from a linoleum block."

Prochnow's copy was a poem written especially for the occasion by Morton Marcus. He was given carte blanche with respect to graphic approach. "I felt the environment the whale lived in offered more emotional possibilities than the animal himself," the designer explains, "so I concentrated on the turbulence of the waters surrounding a whale-shaped void. I wanted to tie in some of the feeling of Japanese design due to their current involvement in whaling." Prochnow's use of wave motifs and negative/positive space relationships reminiscent of oriental woodcuts makes effective exhibition publicity, but it is something of a contradiction in terms for the designer's Japanese-inspired graphics to exalt the whale and warn of its extinction while Japan continues to draw international censure for pursuing an endangered species.

The original 200 posters pulled by Tom Maderos on his Van der Cook press sold so well that an additional 3000 copies were printed offset to be sold by Bookshop Santa Cruz at a lower price. The profits were divided equally among the Museum, Prochnow, Maderos and Marcus, who donated his portion to a save-the-whale fund.

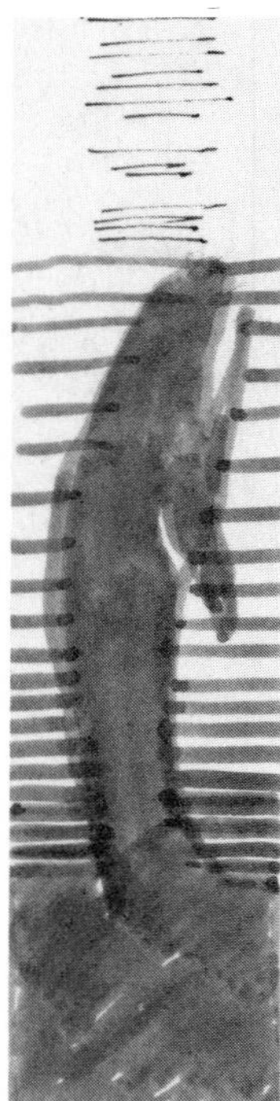

Clients: Bookshop Santa Cruz and Santa Cruz City Museum
Art director/designer: Bill Prochnow
Type designers: Bill Prochnow, Tom Maderos
Copywriter: Morton Marcus
Printers: Tom Maderos (first 200 copies), Tucker Printing (3000 additional copies)
Colors: Black, deep blue
Size: 11″ by 30″

Above and right: preliminary sketches.

Corson Hirschfeld

The drama of a fast-approaching storm over the Great Smoky Mountains made an intriguing subject for photographer Corson Hirschfeld, who shot this threatening panorama in both 4 by 5 and 35mm formats. Back in the darkroom, he found that big enlargements of the 35mm negatives on high-contrast paper recreated the turbulent atmosphere most effectively. A framed print hanging on his studio wall over a period of months received such favorable comment that Hirschfeld and designer William Orr eventually decided to reproduce the print in poster form as a calendar/self-promotion piece.

Rejecting an initial idea to include several smaller frames showing the progression of the storm across the landscape in favor of the striking simplicity of one large image, Hirschfeld and Orr agreed also to position the calendar copy at the bottom of the sheet, where, after the year was over, it could be cut off leaving the photograph intact. Orr's numerical parallelogram echoes the shape of the lowering clouds.

To produce a rich, continuous-tone quality, the designers decided to print the photo double-dot in black and gray with a matte-varnished black border.

Client: Corson Hirschfeld
Design firm: William Orr Design, Cincinnati, OH
Art directors: Corson Hirschfeld, William Orr
Printer: Sanders Printing
Colors: Black and gray
Size: 19" by 29½"

Ivan Illich

When graduate student Judy Anderson was asked to design a poster announcing a lecture at the University of California at Berkeley, she had nothing to work with but the name of the lecturer, Ivan Illich, and the title of his talk, "Medical Nemesis." "I did some research at the library," she recalls, "primarily through the New York Times Book Review, and discovered that Illich's theory is quite unorthodox. He believes that the medical profession is taking us apart and destroying us rather than making us healthy, so I decided to use a death image." Although her design had to conform in size and reproduction method (diazo) to an existing series of posters, she was able to break away from the conventional illustration-at-the-bottom/headline-at-the-top format with a more unified graphic image. "The audience was visually literate," she explains, "so I could use the illustration as the major attention-getter with the copy quite small. I didn't have to 'scream' the message."

Anderson, who had worked for five years as an art director and had returned to the University of California for a Master's degree, used this poster to explore the subtle relationship of message and image in her thesis project. "A series of evolutions was made—from a purely functional, objective treatment to a highly expressive, subjective treatment where the letters/words became important because of their form rather than their meaning," she says. "The degree to which function (in this case the communication of a literal message) and expression of the designer (esthetic decisions) interact determines the richness and effectiveness of the final solution."

The poster was printed in an edition of 25 by the diazo process and was displayed on campus bulletin boards, primarily in the College of Environmental Design.

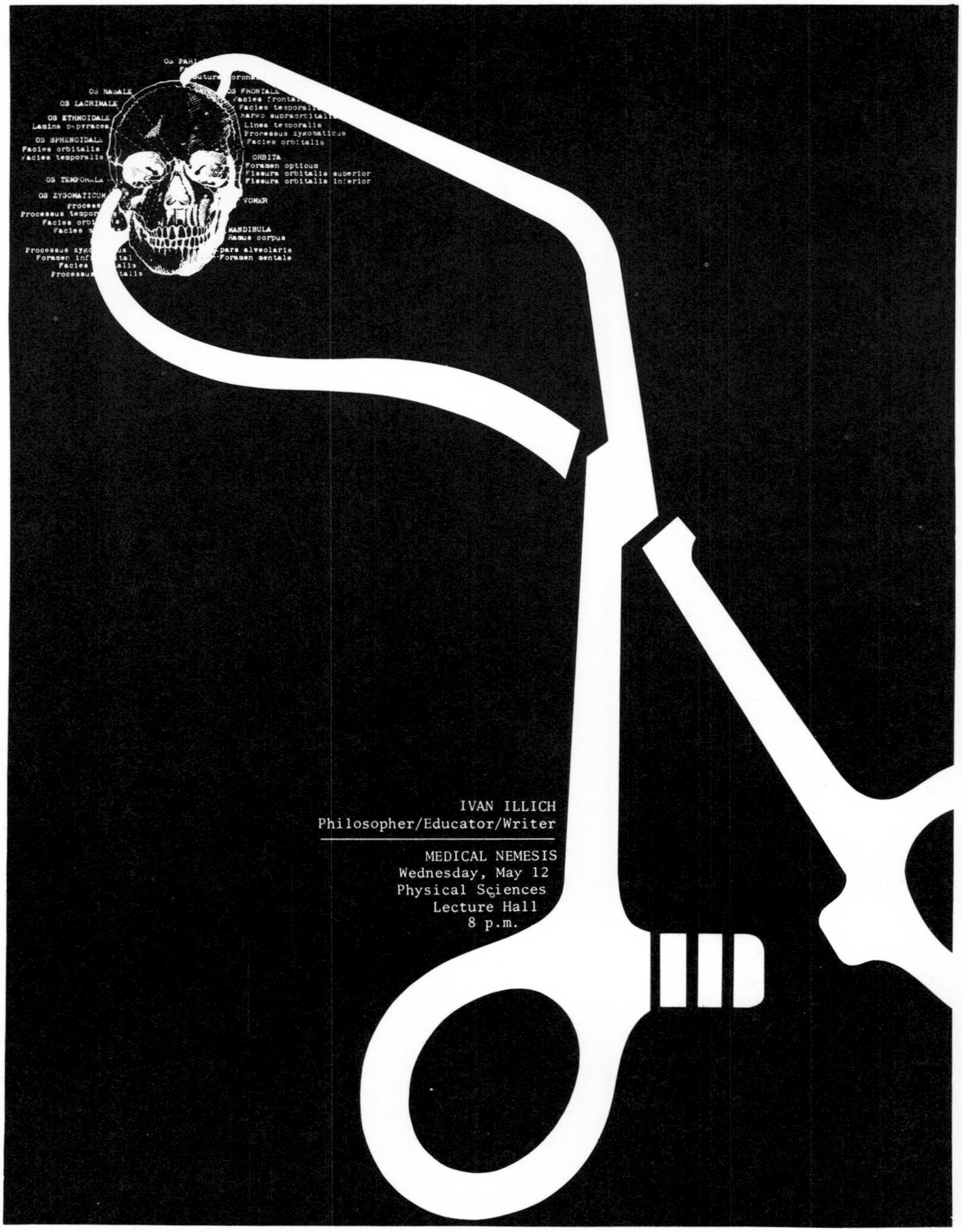

IVAN ILLICH
Philosopher/Educator/Writer

MEDICAL NEMESIS
Wednesday, May 12
Physical Sciences
Lecture Hall
8 p.m.

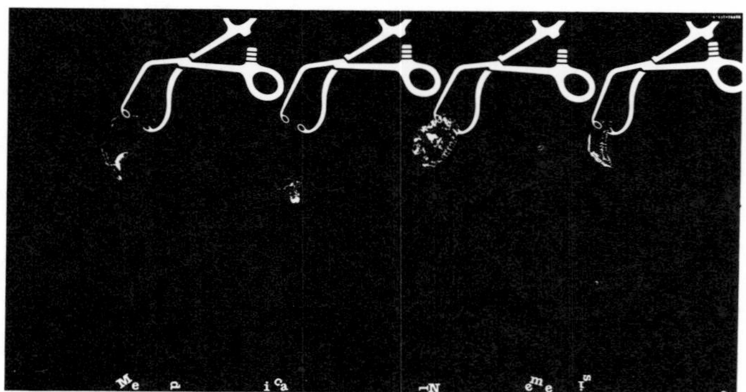

Above: *fifth in a series of variations on Anderson's basic poster design, which she made as illustrations for her thesis project.*

Client: Department of Architecture, University of California, Berkeley
Art director/designer: Judy Anderson
Printer: Berkeley Blueprint
Colors: Black-and-white
Size: 18″ by 24″

St. Heironymous Press

Goines

"Heironymous" is the Latin name for Jerome, a Christian scholar whose revised Latin translation of the Bible formed the basis of the official Vulgate version of the Roman Catholic Church. A man who spent many hours in solitude dedicated to the conscientious production of a masterly work, St. Jerome is a fitting mentor for the proprietor of the St. Heironymous Press, David Lance Goines. Goines also works alone, producing superb posters and carrying out every phase of the operation by himself from original art through camera work, stripping, color separations, mixing inks, and platemaking to printing and trimming. If the responsibility for such thorough involvement is burdensome, Goines is well compensated by the freedom to produce exactly what he wants. He waits upon no art director for approval of his sketches and he knows that the printing will conform to his own rigorous standards.

For a one-man exhibition of his own work at the California Palace of the Legion of Honor, Goines designed a poster featuring a woman's head. He did it for the best and simplest of reasons: he liked it. "It's not particularly representative of anything," he observes. "It's just a nice picture."

His illustration for the "Full Circle" poster, however, *is* representative of something — his own 50-year-old Chandler & Price 10 by 15 press. Asked to design a poster advertising the Full Circle Gallery in Seattle, and given complete liberty with respect to image

Client: California Palace of the Legion of Honor; financed by the Achenbach Foundation
Designer: David Lance Goines
Printer: St. Heironymous Press
Colors: Gray, rose, blue, tan, black, brown
Size: 15″ by 24″

and approach, Goines turned to something near and dear, his own trustworthy machine. It makes an appropriate symbol for a show of vintage graphics and is a just tribute to an old and steadfast partner.

Though Goines was the artist, it was not his press which printed the poster honoring Levon Mosgofian, a highly respected San Francisco printer who has influenced the careers of many young graphic designers. Planned in secret to be presented at a surprise party celebrating Mosgofian's 70th birthday, the poster was printed surreptitiously at night in Mosgofian's own shop, Tea Lautrec Litho, by his sons and pressmen. "We came in at 10 o'clock, worked all night and then cleaned everything up so that he wouldn't find out," relates Goines; "it was particularly neat—like sneaking into somebody's room and doing something without his knowing it." Goines chose the cock as a lively, happy patriarchal image, one which would reflect the personality and status of a man whose opinion is solicited in many a graphic arts controversy and contributes the deciding word in many difficulties and disputes.

Like all of Goines' designs, other examples of which have appeared in previous Casebooks, these posters are expertly printed in mixed to match colors on high quality stock. Goines reports that "Levon was knocked out" by his unusually large birthday card and Goines' own exhibition poster sold out at the museum in two weeks.

Client: Full Circle Gallery
Designer: David Lance Goines
Printer: St. Heironymous Press
Colors: Tan, ivory, black, rust, gray, gold
Size: 18″ by 24″

Levon

Client: Denis and Seth Mosgofian
Designer: David Lance Goines
Printer: Tea Lautrec Litho
Colors: Blue, brown, bone, black
Size: 18″ by 24″

Although New Yorkers may think it impossible for animals of this kind to exist in a subway environment, the fact is that the Frog and the Gecko have taken up residence at the Pelham Parkway station. Designed by Peter Bradford and the third-year students in his class in conceptual design at the School of Visual Arts, the posters were produced as part of an imaginative if modest subway renovation project funded by Exxon. The project, called "Platforms for Design," was organized by three private, non-profit groups concerned with brightening the urban landscape—the Arts and Business Council, the Public Arts Council, and the Municipal Art Society. Four Design firms were invited to participate in the project and asked to create a graphic program which would change a monotonous, dismal subway station into a more attractive place. The designers could choose any station and graphic solution they liked as long as the graphics related in some way to the institution or community above ground which the station served. Each firm was allotted $5000 to cover design fees, material costs, fabrication and installation, as well as several months' poster-space rental in those stations where the designs made use of the advertising billboards.

Stimulated by the prospect of making an exciting visual impact on ordinarily drab surroundings, Bradford decided to concentrate his efforts on the Pelham station, known as the Bronx Zoo stop,

The Gecko

a park entrance which he considered just as important as the zoo's main gates. Besides acting as a link with one of the city's most popular institutions, the site had another advantage: the entire length of the 500′ platform was immediately visible to both uptown and downtown riders.

The students' solution was to paint the dingy, graffiti-ridden green of the corrugated platform walls with an abstract rolling landscape in two shades of gray. Each of the 34 5′ by 4′ advertisements was replaced by one of 14 huge, brilliantly-colored animal posters dramatizing lesser-known details and images of various species in the zoo. Basing their designs on scientific data supplied by Mary Anne McLean, Bradford and his class devised simple, instantly recognizable dramatic shapes that would make an immediate impact on even the most distracted subway rider. "You can look across and see the big images," Bradford explains, "and behind you there are other images with type to read. It works at different distances."

Because of the low budget, the posters were silkscreened in a limited selection of colors and only 20 to 30 impressions were pulled of each subject. Their success is undisputed. "People tried to remove them and take them home," Bradford reports. Failing that, they walked the entire length of the platform reading the information. "They even let trains go by," Bradford says with obvious satisfaction, "and in that part of town, there's a 15-to-20-minute wait."

Client: Arts and Business Council; Public Arts Council/Municipal Art Society of New York; Exxon Corp.
Art director: Peter Bradford
Designers: Ronald Finkelstein (gecko); Kevin Larkin (frog)
Copywriter: Mary Anne McLean
Printer: Tricia Deck/Purrington Impressions
Colors: Peacock blue on silver (gecko); green on orange (frog)
Size: 5′ by 4′

View of open-air elevated Pelham Parkway station platform showing "The Gecko" and other Bradford posters in place.

The story of Inês de Castro, a legendary beauty of 14th-century Portugal, is rich with the drama of forbidden love, political intrigue and murderous vengeance—just the sort of tale to inspire an ambitious librettist or talented composer. Consequently, it was this slice of Portuguese history that John Collinge, general manager of the Baltimore Opera Company, chose as the basis for a new American opera, to be commissioned in honor of the U.S. Bicentennial. The book and music were completed late in 1974 by, respectively, Bernard Stambler and Thomas Pasatieri; by the end of 1975 artists and production staff had been engaged.

To generate publicity about the new production, the Baltimore Opera Company sponsored a poster contest open to all local graphic designers. The prize was to be $250 and the time allowance approximately six months from announcement until completion date. A brief synopsis of the plot was supplied. Otherwise, there were no restrictions or production requirements, a happy circumstance which offered the contestants unusual freedom.

"I researched the original love story, and it seemed essential that I use Dona Inês de Castro as the central image for my poster," explains Bob Helsley, whose entry was chosen as the winner by Collinge and art directors from two Baltimore advertising agencies. Basing his illustration on paintings of 14th-century Portuguese costumes, jewelry

and lace work, Helsley rendered his final art in the rose and purple of theatrical lighting gels against a black background. The bluish tinge of Inês's skin subtly suggests her doom; the gold outline of the arched columnar frame places the story in its early Renaissance setting.

Four months later, money became available through a private grant to have the poster printed as promotion for the opera's world premiere. "Several printers turned the job down," Helsley recalls, "and an expensive printer had to be selected to reproduce the original as closely as possible. I had painted the poster large—about 24″ by 30″—in tempera and gouache. The letters were airbrushed or presstype and there were no separations since it had originally been intended as a one-of-a-kind piece." The final job was a seven-times-through-the-press production to allow for four colors, gold, matte black and varnish. Two hundred copies were signed by Helsley and Pasatieri and sold to help defray the printing costs.

Client: Baltimore Opera/Lyric Theater
Art director/designer: Bob Helsley
Printer: King Printing
Colors: Four-color, plus gold, matte black, varnish
Size: 20″ by 26″

Left and above: preliminary sketches; below: program cover.

Ines de Castro

Baltimore Opera Silver Jubilee Season
Lyric Theatre, April 1, 3 & 5 1976

Deity, Worship & Death

McRay Magleby's pyramidal triumvirate symbolizing deity, worship and death is so elegantly simple, so brilliantly appropriate to the theme that it deserves a much wider audience than the one for which it was originally intended. Designed to advertise an annual symposium on comparative world religions, sponsored by the Religious Studies Center at Brigham Young University in Provo, Utah, it was displayed on campus bulletin boards to be seen from a distance of approximately three feet. It is a viewing space which Magleby, a part-time teacher (in advanced graphic design) and full-time employee of the firm Graphic Communications, is used to dealing with. "Graphic Communications," he explains, "was originally the art department for the university press, but it now also functions as an in-house agency for the whole university." In that capacity, the firm is responsible for designing not only books but also brochures, posters and other printed material representing Brigham Young. In addition to a basic staff of five, it employs six or seven part-time student designers, some of whom are salaried and some of whom intern for credit but not pay. One of these able apprentices, Mike Cooper, working from Magleby's original tissue rendering, carried out the final production of the poster. To keep within the $150 budget, 100 copies of the design were silkscreened in only two colors —orange (the striated rectangle) and brown (the type). The motif was also used on the symposium program and on the cover of a collection of conference speeches.

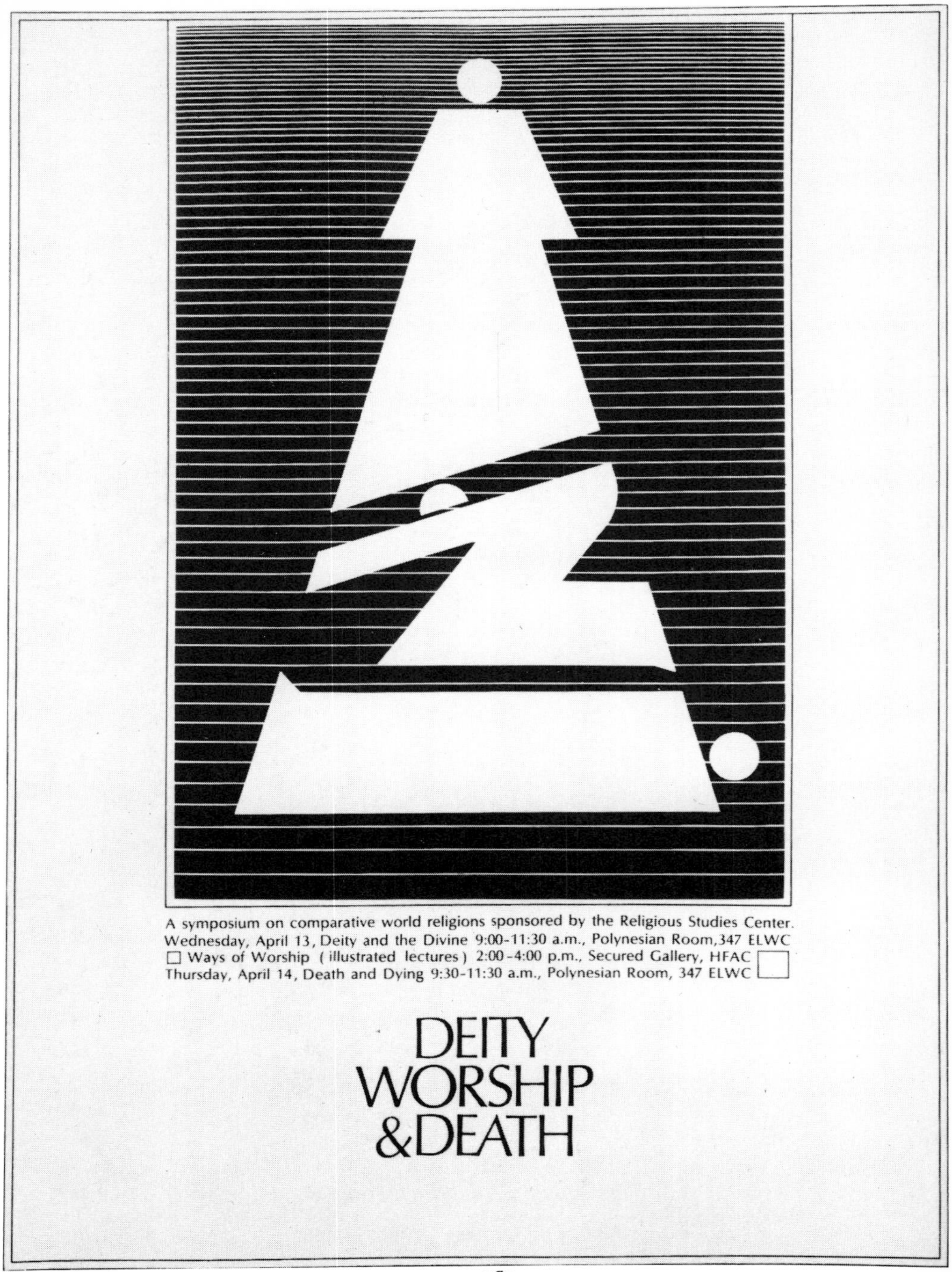

A symposium on comparative world religions sponsored by the Religious Studies Center.
Wednesday, April 13, Deity and the Divine 9:00-11:30 a.m., Polynesian Room, 347 ELWC
☐ Ways of Worship (illustrated lectures) 2:00-4:00 p.m., Secured Gallery, HFAC ☐
Thursday, April 14, Death and Dying 9:30-11:30 a.m., Polynesian Room, 347 ELWC ☐

DEITY
WORSHIP
&DEATH

Client: Religious Studies Center, Brigham Young University
Design firm: Graphic Communications, Provo, UT
Art director/designer: McRay Magleby
Illustrators: McRay Magleby, Mike Cooper
Copywriter: Spencer W. Palmer
Printer: Graphic Communications
Colors: Orange, dark brown
Size: 20″ by 26″

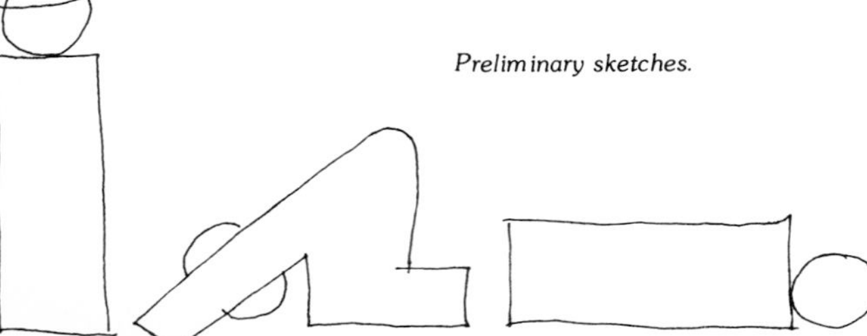

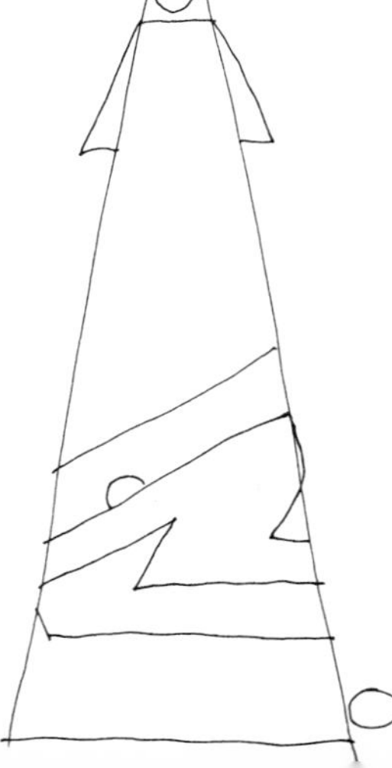

Preliminary sketches.